Literacy on 1

Also available from Bloomsbury

Education, Policy and Social Justice, James Avis

Literacy on the Left
Reform and Revolution

Andrew Lambirth

BLOOMSBURY

LONDON • NEW DELHI • NEW YORK • SYDNEY

Bloomsbury Academic
An imprint of Bloomsbury Publishing Plc

50 Bedford Square   175 Fifth Avenue
London   New York
WC1B 3DP   NY 10010
UK   USA

www.bloomsbury.com

First published by Continuum International Publishing Group 2011
Paperback edition first published 2012

British Library Cataloguing-in-Publication Data
A catalogue record for this book is available from the British Library.

ISBN: HB: 978-1-4411-0698-8
PB: 978-1-4411-9413-8

Library of Congress Cataloging-in-Publication Data
Lambirth, Andrew, 1959–
Literacy on the left: reform and revolution / Andrew Lambirth.
p. cm.
Includes bibliographical references and index.
ISBN 978-1-4411-0698-8 (hardcover) – ISBN 978-1-4411-5547-4 (ebook (pdf))
1. Literacy–Political aspects. 2. Right and left (Political science). 3. Ideology.
I. Title.
LC149.L224 2010
302.2'244–dc22 2010033858

Typeset by Newgen Imaging Systems Pvt Ltd, Chennai, India
Printed and bound in Great Britain

To Joyce: for a mother's love and for the many political discussions I had with you as a child; a rich education indeed.

Contents

Acknowledgements

This book could not have been written without my experience of working with children in primary schools in London and in Kent. It was they who provided me with my own initial education in the way schooling in literacy and English operates in the United Kingdom. I will be forever grateful for the experiences they provided and hope that I may have contributed in some way to their interest in reading and writing.

I have been greatly helped in writing this book by the many scholars I have cited and quoted throughout. I found Robin Small's *Marx and Education* extremely insightful and useful in assisting my academic understanding of the work of Marx. Evidence of Small's contribution can be found throughout the book. I must also acknowledge Alan Woods's contribution through his writing in providing insights from a revolutionary Marxist perspective and offering a practical alternative to academic Marxist positions.

I found books from the 1970s extremely useful and enlightening. I hope that there may be more texts published that take the politics of education and literacy as their main subject in the near future. Castles and Wustenburg's book *The Education of the Future: An Introduction to the Theory and Practice of Socialist Education* continues to offer guidance on education from a left perspective; it, too, played a major role in influencing the arguments in this book. I would also like to acknowledge the work of Chris Searle. With the published work of his students, he offers an enlightening and alternative form of critical literacy. Hilary Janks has also been influential in enabling me to critique what I call post-structuralist versions of critical literacy. Her book *Literacy and Power* is a stimulating read and provides an excellent example of this form of literacy practice.

I would also like to acknowledge my many discussions and debates with colleagues and students about literacy. These discussions have been vital in working towards understanding the role of politics in literacy education.

Last, but by no means least, I want to acknowledge the love and support of Helen, Joyce and Alan.

Introduction

This is a book about literacy education, ideology and political selfhood. It studies what it means to teach literacy on the left of politics. I have written this book because I want to encourage readers to look again at their own ideas on literacy education and schooling and to plot their position on the political spectrum that makes power relations in human societies. This may not be a comfortable task as it entails questioning one's own values, but the book is built on the premise of the importance of knowing where one stands as an educator, teacher, parent or indeed anyone who is interested in modern-day society and how schools should teach children to read, write, speak and listen. It asks its readers to re-attune the nature of their gaze on the most seemingly mundane elements of literacy schooling – the resources; the interchange between teacher and child; language-use; the class group-ings; the content of the curriculum and so on – asking the simple question: 'Who gains from this approach?' This book will address issues of power, domination and the complex dialectical role that language and literacy schooling have in reproducing inequalities, but also its potential in offering the means to empowerment and hope within the context of capitalist societies. I want the book to disturb its readers intellectually by demanding answers about how their hopes and fears, beliefs, expectations, sensitivities, and values, sculpt their views on what should happen to children in schools and what that means in terms of the broader political world and its future.

For me, it was after reading Basil Bernstein (1996) around ten years ago that I found myself forced to face the political realities of my own practice within my career trajectory as primary school teacher, teacher educator, and academic in the present economic system. Looking at education and literacy schooling through the analytical lens that Bernstein offered made my professional and, indeed, my personal world change forever. His brilliant and penetrating perspectives on, for example, teaching being a form of cultural relay and the social class assumptions of pedagogy, made me ask myself about these notions' significance to patterns of achievement and underachievement in schools and my role as a self-proclaimed teacher on the political 'left'.

I have always believed that the daily task of someone in education is to empower students by providing them with the intellectual and practical skills to analyse the world and to be able to make decisions with an informed perspective; to introduce students to the ideas and works of humanity that will challenge and excite. Education is about social justice and its contribution to providing people with the knowledge to form fair and democratic societies and to flourish and thrive therein.

An account like this of the aims and functions of education contrasts with instrumentalist approaches that prioritize schooling for the support of the economic viability of capitalist society. Yet, those who have held views similar to mine – those who consider themselves on the left in education – are faced with a problem that is fundamental to the thesis of this book. This problem will be confronted as part of an examination into the ideological background of literacy practice: that is, the continuing pattern of under-achievement, linked to the socio-economic background or social class of those in school. Hatcher (2006) sets the scene starkly:

> If you want to know how well a child will do in school, ask how much its parents earn. The fact remains, after more than 50 years of the welfare state and several decades of comprehensive education, that family wealth is the single best predictor of success in the school system . . . social class, defined in terms of socio-economic status correlates closely with attain-ment in school. (p. 202)

There is overwhelming evidence that economic inequality is mirrored by inequalities in achievement in school (i.e., Smith et al. 1997, Beckett 2000, McCallum and Redhead 2000, Thomas 2000, DfED 2000, OECD 2001, Ennals 2004, DfES 2004, DfES 2006, Hirsch 2007). There is much research and there are many well-meaning reports that highlight this persistent problem. Yet, I find myself struck by the nature of many of their recommenda-tions. In these reports, poverty is often construed as an unfortunate but inevitable part of society, whose effects can be mediated and lessened by a number of reforms, often at the level of the classroom. Hirsch's (2007) report for the Child Poverty Action Group, for example, acknow-ledges the inextricable link between poverty and educational achievement. The report recommends creating environments outside the mainstream school which foster 'new learning relations' (p. 7) with adult staff and to offer more positive homework opportunities. Hirsch does concede that this will not improve all the social differences that breed underachievement for disadvantaged children, but he believes it will begin a process of change. This approach is not unusual, as there are a number of projects around the world that attempt similar ways of improving the lot of the working class in schools in affluent countries. This often involves changing relationships between teachers and students; redesigning the curriculum or pedagogical methods and altering approaches to discipline and behaviour management (van der Berg 2008). These attempts to affect change seem informed by a belief that high achievement in schools is mainly due to students making the right life-choices – choosing to be good and to work hard.

However, the problems of socio-economic status, social class and poverty remain a constant that causes the disadvantage in schools. Levin (2004) points out, summarizing from evidence from the United States, that 'sustained improvement over time in high poverty schools is rare despite claims from studies in exceptional schools' (p. 47). Gillborn and Mirza's (2000) review of research in this area shows that social class continues to have overwhelming significance but receives far less attention in policy than other issues concerning equality, like race and gender. Indeed, it has been argued, that social class has currently no place in the language of education policy (Ball 2008). The terms 'disadvantaged', 'dispossessed' and the 'socially excluded' are always the preferred nomenclatures for 'working class'. Despite this, class has been seen to intersect with race and gender inequalities, which has the effect of multiplying disadvantage (Ball 2008). Ennals (2004) concluded that the largest class divide in education in the industrialized world is to be found in the United Kingdom. The report showed that the attainment gap between the poor and the better off was evident at 22 months of a child's life and became larger as children grew older. It also reported that young people from unskilled backgrounds were over five times less likely to enter higher education than those from professional backgrounds.

Efforts to erase this record of disadvantage have been largely unsuccessful on any long-term basis. The history of education policy reveals 'dual and contradictory policy imperatives that derive from the aspirations and fears of the middle classes, on the one hand, and the limited participation and underachievement of various sections of the working class on the other' (Ball 2008:96–97). Efforts to assist the poor and the working class to do better in school through reform have often been led by a mixture of policy, philanthropy, voluntarism and the contribution from faith schools. In many cases, the middle class have benefited far more from reform in education than those who were the intended recipients (Jones 2003, Ball 2008).

This persistent pattern of working-class underachievement and the relative frail impact of reform in over 70 years of education has been the spur to many academics and teachers to try to understand this phenomena (i.e., Bernstein 1996, Bourdieu and Passeron 1977, Apple 2004). Bernstein's work and its intellectual effects on my own teaching reawakened a desire to explore the politics of what I was doing as a teacher pursuing my, perhaps, naïve ideals, but also to reexamine the work of others whom I had not, until then, attended to with the same methodology. This led me to reconsider the politics and sociology of pedagogy and 'look up' from the purely cognitive and linguistic preoccupations and implications of the practice that I read and advocated, to see its cultural and political impact both in its micro and macro aspects (Lambirth 2006). It is for this reason that the argument of this book is premised on the view that patterns of poor achievement in schools are not an aberration, but are integral products of the way schools are organized in present socio-economic conditions. I discuss this in detail in Chapter 1 when I introduce the role of Marxism as a radical guide to understanding how education functions. My intention is that readers experience this 'process of reformulation of perspective' with their own practice, using these and other political philosophies and principles that I intend to describe and examine.

Vygotsky (1997) famously wrote that:

> Pedagogics is never and was never politically indifferent, since, willingly or unwillingly, through its own work on the psyche, it has always adopted a particular social pattern, political line, in accordance with the dominant social class that has guided its interests. (p. 348)

Vygotsky was a Marxist. This is an important position in the book's examination of the politics of pedagogy, exploring what literacy on the left is, and can be. Marxism will be presented as the extreme example of left politics and will be contrasted with other forms of left politics. Educational policy and its politics will feature strongly in this book as I examine the political motivations of strategies in the United Kingdom and the United States for the promotion of particular forms of literacy education. However, this book also looks at the ideas concerning the pedagogy of literacy from within the educational establishment itself – the schools, the universities and associations – which often inform and mediate the way policy is realized in school.

This book is not a history, but an analysis of what it might mean to teach literacy from a politically left perspective – is it indeed possible, and if so, what does it look like? I expect readers to be surprised by what is revealed along the way. It will mean tackling political theory that forms the background to educational discourses and has such a pivotal role in what goes on in school. The book explores a complex subject and cannot hope to cover all aspects of its field. I will inevitably omit the names and ideas of those who some may feel essential to the arguments, yet I intend to offer what I feel will provide important insights into the politics of literacy education in the twenty-first century.

In the remainder of this introductory chapter, I will describe notions of left and right in politics, discussing the derivation of the terms and how this may relate to approaches to literacy education. I then go on to introduce perspectives on educational ideology that will be central to the subject of this book. Intrinsic to notions of ideology in education is the trajectory of education policy from the nineteenth century onwards. The discussion is to give readers a legislative context for the conceptualization of literacy. Lastly in this chapter, I present a range of definitions of literacy that will prepare readers for the political and philosophical background to approaches to literacy education which this book analyses.

What's Left?

It seems sensible to begin with a discussion of what I mean broadly by the 'left' in politics and education and, consequently what the 'right' is, too. Political positions are often classified this way within organizations and institutions where the potential for politics is explicit. Of course, politics is arguably everywhere. As a famous revolutionary and politician once said: 'Politics fills the air; it is not possible to live outside of politics, without politics, any more than one can live without air' (Trotsky [1924]1973:282). Politics is the complex of relationships between people in a society and as such is involved in all we do in the world. One may not want to believe this or knowingly engage in these politics, but one does, even if this means acceptance, consent and compliance in the network of power relations that make political systems in both the micro and the macro of human organizations and cultures. One's actions in public and private life are informed and controlled by an ideology. There are no neutral positions or apolitical actions. This is true of what happens in classrooms and in this book.

In many public and private groupings of humans, the beliefs and actions of those therein are often classified as being 'left' or 'right' political perspectives. Traditionally, the left includes social democrats, social liberals, socialists, communists, postmodernists, environmentalists, and anarchists.

The right includes conservatives, fascists, monarchists and nationalists (van Gosse 2005, Reuss 2000, Berman 2007). However, the political spectrum of ideological perspectives spirals in. Political parties, like the UK's Labour Party (traditionally a left of centre party) or Conservative party (a right of centre party), have their own left- and right-wing factions. Other institutions, like the church have left-wing and right-wing members, and in education there are teachers and education commentators who are thought to be right-wing or left-wing in their outlook. To complicate things further, in both the left-wing and right-wing of these factions there are also extremes – the ultra left and the ultra right.

The left and right in politics partly derive from the political classification in eighteenth-century France, specifically the French legislative assembly of 1791. The king was still the formal head of government. Traditional royalists, known as the Feuillants, sat to the right of the king in the chamber and the radical Montagnards sat to his left. The right of the chamber supported the ancient regime and aristocratic feudalism that was teetering on the brink of destruction, while the left was in favour of republicanism, the new middle class and civil liberties (Knapp and Wright 2006). There is no space here for a thorough history of left and right politics with all their complexities, but one may wish to argue that the modern left is often still associated with the desire to change society through forms of democratic intervention of either the masses in revolution, or through radical, but gradual parliamentary reform. These changes and interventions are often thought to be the role of the democratic state. It is this belief in a muscular democratic state that is the chief defining element of left politics and distinguishes it from the right. Through one of these means, the left have advocated a more equal society brought about by better education, full employment and free healthcare. The right, on the other hand, champion a conservative approach, a belief in the righteousness of present systems, less state interventionism and confidence in the free market to affect desired social outcomes in education and employment (Davies 1996).

A further derivation of the left and right and one that may help an understanding of this spectrum of political belief comes from when the young Karl Marx was a student in Germany in the 1800s. At the time, followers of the philosopher Georg Wilhelm Friedrich Hegel split into two distinct factions, one known as the Left Hegelians, or the Young Hegelians, and the other as the Right Hegelians. When Hegel was a young man he had welcomed the French Revolution, but later in life he took a more complaisant position favouring reasonableness and acceptance of the world as one finds it (Wheen 2006). For Hegel, all that was real was rational. The Right

Hegelians took this to mean that the present state and political system were real and therefore rational and beyond reproach. However, for the Left Hegelians, his work on dialectics also indicated that all that is real will *become* irrational and that everything that exists will perish. It was this position that formed the revolutionary significance of Hegel's philosophy (Sewell 2007) and made some of the Young Hegelians left-wing and revolutionary in outlook. They recognized the potential for change in all things and consequently they foresaw the demise of their present regime, and all regimes in the future, as a means for human society to develop.

The arguments within the left of politics have a long history of just how to effect lasting social change and a desire for equality within society. Is it achieved through reform or revolution (Luxemburg 1970, Woods 2008, Dietrich 2006)? Importantly for this book – what is the role of schooling and education in affecting these changes? Can schooling be instrumental in creating equality? On the other hand, will the creation of equality produce the circumstances conducive to real schooling and education? By examining the history of education policy, it is possible to discern the divisions in ideology that manifest themselves among educationalists, politicians and commentators. But first I want to discuss how I shall be using the concepts of ideology and discourse.

The Ideology and Discourse

How one conceives the aims and functions of education is thought to be guided by ideology. An ideology is a set of beliefs regarded as self-evidently true. It creates a basis for certainty about the world and the structures and organizations that exit therein (Lemke 1995). An ideology can have an overwhelming influence (Eagleton 2000) and the ideas within an ideology are based upon what groups believe are right and wrong and what is 'common-sense'. Ideologies arise because of individual and group histories and experiences of social and economic relations and conditions (Hill 2001).

An educational ideology will influence everything that happens in environments where there are forms of pedagogy. It makes the discourse about teaching and learning and the conceptualization of childhood and development and, what is more, in so doing, it will appear as being the truth to all that hold that ideology. The meaning of 'discourse' here is based on the view that language, whether spoken or written, is a form of social practice and, consequently, is formed and controlled by an ideology. What we say or write is always determined by social contexts and their conventions. How we use language is closely controlled by social forces within the different environments where linguistic interchange occurs. Even in the most intimate and personal surroundings, where we feel ourselves to be at our most individual, our language is still subject to these social rules (Fairclough 2001). As Gee (2001) explains:

> It is sometimes helpful to say that it is not individuals who speak and act, but rather historically and socially defined discourses speak to each other through individuals. The individual instantiates, gives body to, a discourse every time he acts or speaks. (p. 3)

Indeed, Foucault (1979a, b) saw language-use and cultural practices as being dialogical. For Foucault, discourse is the means by which institutions and cultures with particular ideological positions exert their power 'through a process of definition and exclusion, intelligibility and legitimacy' (Storey 2001:78). Discourses are soaked in ideological unwritten rules and assumptions that actually define what it is possible to say. Foucault contended that the discourse produces a reality through the language used to describe and explain specific contexts and environments. Therefore, educational ideologies, like other forms of ideologies, are often passionately held and profoundly influence the behaviour of those in the classrooms, both teachers and learners on the right or the left of the political spectrum.

This position on discourse and ideology has political tensions and connotations itself. There are many who do not conceptualize human thought and action as always being hewn from an ideology. Instead, a set of ideas held by particular groups of people can be seen as a source of bias and irrationality. In education, the 1980s and 1990s saw a constant stream of accusations of ideological bias of teachers in their methods and from teachers about government ministers (Pollard 1996). From a negative perspective, ideology is seen as a form of 'false consciousness' (Larrain 1979). It can distort social reality and conceal social contradictions and conflicts. Ideologies have the power to fool people into accepting the interests of the dominant groups. On the other hand, it is also seen as benign. Seen this way, our consciousness is inevitably wrought from the material conditions within which we live. We must accept that our social being sculpts human nature and therefore society creates our consciousness. This means that societies can be constructed that beget a human race able to reach its full potential for intellectual and physical greatness. It follows that within our present social domains all we do is influenced by ideology and is inscribed in the discourse. To deny this simply reveals an inability to grasp the source of one's behaviour and ideas.

An educational ideology will possess a theory for schools of: discipline and order; knowledge, its content and structure; learning and the learner's role; teaching and the teacher's role; resources appropriate for teaching; organization of learning situations; assessment that learning has taken place; aims, objectives and outcomes; parents and the parents' role; locations appropriate for learning and power and distribution (Meighan and Siraj-Blatchford 1998). As politics involves the allocation, distribution and control of resources (Hill 2001), how all of this is done in schools will be of great importance to different groups within society. Those who control these resources will wield enormous power and influence and potentially command and determine the futures of individuals in different communities.

When talking of the politics of literacy one needs to focus on both matters of state jurisdiction concerning the making, applying, interpreting and enforcing law that pertains to literacy and the politics of power and conflict. By this, I mean the processes and settings in which literacy skills are transmitted and acquired and the agencies responsible for defining and promoting literacy within society (Lankshear and Lawler 1987).

A Short History of English Education Policy

Like some others (Hill 2001, Cole 2006, Ball 2008), I view the history of education policy through the lens of social class and this brief history reflects this perspective. In Chapter 1, I shall try to define social class in detail, but until then I will assume an understanding that by class I mean groups of people who share a similar social position in terms of power and status in society and certain political and cultural characteristics.

State education began to emerge in the nineteenth century. It developed in response to an increase in the population within urban areas. A new industrialized society emerged. From 1844 until 1944 education was dominated by class-based policy (Kelly 2000). Alongside the growing urban working class came a burgeoning new middle class of managers and professionals who, recognizing themselves as a class with their own needs and aspirations, demanded an education policy both for themselves and for the working class that was in their employ or stewardship (Simon 1994).

Early state intervention in education came mainly in the shape of teacher training, the nature of which was designed to fashion teachers who might act as role-models for their working-class students. The evidence suggests

(Perkin 1969, Best 1973, Hill 2001) that nineteenth-century education policy was deliberately shaped in a way to perpetuate class differences. There was certainly no policy concern for equal opportunities. Ball (2008) quotes Mathew Arnold who sat on the Newcastle Commission into Elementary Schools in 1861: 'The education of each class in society has, or ought to have its ideal, determined by the wants of that class, and by its destination' ([1864]1969, p. 112). The Clarenden Commission of 1864 on public schools further illustrates this. The writers recommend that private schools like Eton and Harrow should ensure the reproduction of the cultures and manners of the old and new upper classes (Ball 2008). In addition, The Schools Inquiry Commission 1868 (Taunton) that studied grammar schools suggested three grades of fee-paying schools that excluded the working class and were best-suited to the different fractions of the middle class with curricular to match. As a result of these commissions a tri-partite system emerged – elementary schools for the working class, secondary for the middle class and private schools for the ruling class.

It was not until the 1944 Education Act that free schooling for all was introduced. Yet, even then, the division between types of schools – grammar and secondary modern – was arguably modelled by a will for a class-divided society, where children were segregated by socio-economic status and the students' different 'types of mind', as it was described then. Yet many reformers at the time were satisfied by what the Act offered – a discourse of hope (Jones 2003). There appeared to be a broad social-democratic consensus upon what the aims and functions of education should be, one of which was to create a better and fairer society. The 11 plus exam was seen as a way to tolerate some working-class children's social mobility into grammar schools and onward into university and the professions.

I think it is important to pause here, as it should be remembered that postwar reform in education policy only came, arguably, because of the radicalization of the masses in Western Europe at the end of a tragic, bloody, and arduous Second World War (Grant 2002). The coming to power of the first majority Labour government in the United Kingdom reflected this radical turn. The working class were determined that never again should they return to the poverty and privation of the interwar years. Yet, according to the Marxist commentator, Grant (2002), capitalism was saved by the reformist and Communist leaders who made pacts with other parties who were committed to capitalism, to create the conditions for an economic upswing that would last until the 1970s.

The 1950s have been called the golden age of British capitalism (Hobsbawn 1994). A harmonization existed between countries united against communism in the east and wages rose with the increase in production. The strong economy could afford a general consensus about the importance of education in society (Jones 2003).

Despite the radical nature of the postwar reforms, in the 1950s and 1960s a series of reports and research (Gurney-Dixon 1954, Glass 1954, Floud et al. 1956) highlighted class divisions and how the divided system in education was reproducing unambiguous class differences in attainment in schools. The middle class predominantly attended the grammar schools and only a highly selected number of working-class students were given access to the same schools (Ball 2008). During this time, The Labour Party began to construct an argument against education selection. In doing so, it heralded a change in the reformist-left's perspectives. Its radical programme of nationalization of the commanding heights of the economy – transport, and heavy industry – was the way it had intended to shape Britain's economic future. However, as Jones (2003) has shown, the left's 'path to Socialism' was diverted away from a nationalization project towards a future where education was to play a far more influential role. Crosland (1956) advocated a model of left and socialist politics that highlighted aims that included equal opportunity in education and those:

> . . . that increased the social capacities of working class people, freed them from dependence, and prioritized opportunity to the point where people's occupations and destinies no longer corresponded to their social origins. Such a social order characterized both by mobility and by the equal sharing of goods like education and health, was Crosland's alternative to nationalisation. (Jones 2003:50)

Marxists in postwar Britain (Grant 2002), while supporting the reforms that improved the conditions of working-class people, were also grimly aware of the lost opportunity in 1945 to transform society by removing capitalism forever. For them, the reformists on the left had consciously betrayed workers and exposed their own class allegiances. They had not taken the occasion to galvanize the radicalization and mood of working-class people who had demanded change at the end of the war and would have supported revolution above reform.

The masses desired a fundamental change and expressed this by voting Labour. Had the Labour leaders wanted it, they could have carried through the socialist transformation of society through parliament.

Nothing could have stopped them. But, of course, they had no intention of doing anything of the sort. (Grant 2002:201)

For the Marxist left, any reforms made by the Labour Party within a capitalist-led society would ultimately always lead to the demise of working-class hopes and aspirations, particularly as an economic upswing turns inevitably into a slump. Crosland's move to concentrate on education as a way to working-class emancipation was arguably a Labour right-wing initiative. It became a symptom that contributed to the repositioning of the Party's 'road to Socialism'. It took the political heat away from the need to control the commanding heights of the economy towards policy initiatives that were in the relative periphery of a working-class party's potential power. The role of relatively radical education reform as a right-wing counter-socialist measure is a phenomenon that I will say more about later and informs the conclusions of this book.

In 1964, the Labour Party was reelected, and introduced Circular 10/65, which asked that local education authorities provide plans for a comprehensive system of education. This occurred side-by-side with more progressive and child-centred teaching approaches in schools. There were no national plans to direct the replacement of grammar schools with comprehensive schools as there appeared to be a lack of enthusiasm and political will from the politicians (Ball 2008), so progress was slow. Furthermore, as the changes began to occur, the backlash from the political right began (Black papers, 1969–77).

The 1976 Ruskin College speech made by Labour Party leader, James Callaghan, occurred just after capitalism had suffered an international economic crisis and the aims and functions of education began to be redefined once again (Hill 2001). Education needed to serve the economy more than by simply attempting to encourage individual fulfilment. This would mean government bodies issuing strong guidance to teachers and professionals in a way not witnessed since 1944. This echoed the warnings from Marxists (Grant 2002), whose understanding of capitalist economics led them to predict the continuing pattern of boom and slump and, consequently, the heavy price that working-class people would pay.

From 1979 and the election of the right-wing Conservative government, schools were introduced to the direct forces of markets and competition. A National Curriculum was introduced, more-or-less, alongside compulsory national tests and the publication of league tables (Hill 2001). From now on, funding for schools would be driven by recruitment heralding the encouragement of a diversity of provision by, for example, the introduction of grant-maintained schools. Competition would be the incentive for schools to make 'improvements' and attract the choices of parents. The league tables provided 'market information' for the choosers and this market environment led to forms of management in schools that turned to business models to ensure efficient budget maximization (Ball 2008).

New Labour's election victory in 1997 led to education policy that has been described (Hill 2001) as partly a continuing social democratic objective to extend equal opportunities. Rentoul (1997) disputes this, describing the Blair government's policies as 'instilling discipline and responsibility' (p. 431) rather than equality. New Labour sustained a course followed by their Conservative predecessors of a 'back to basics' traditionalism and the continued development of the market's influence on the functioning of schools. This included an increase in privatization, diversity and a hierarchy of schools (Hill 2001).

In 1998, the National Literacy Strategy (DfES 1998) was introduced as a way of improving the literacy of primary school children. This was a result of a number of reports (Ofsted 1996a, 1996b) that highlighted deficiencies in teaching in this area of the curriculum. Literacy in schools appeared now to be conceptualized as the main aim of formal educational processes in primary school settings, rather than as simply an essential tool for accessing other learning (Lankshear and Knobel 2003). The strategy formed an important component of the thrust back to traditionalism and a unitary and monocultural definition and approach to literacy and its teaching. This model was peddled as children's entitlement in schools as a means to feed the economy by increasing young people's ability to compete in the labour market. Literacy had taken 'centre-stage' in the battles over educational ideology and I shall now introduce some definitions and arguments about literacy that form the hub of ideological battles between the left and right and that will recur in different forms and contexts as the book progresses.

Language and Literacy

The common view of literacy, and one that is often discussed unproblematically, is that it is made up of a set of skills and competences that provide the ability to use written language (McGuinness 1998). In this view, literacy is unvarying and unitary in nature and can be given to children in schools as a package of skills. Although it is acknowledged that the uses of literacy will depend on social, economic and political factors that may affect the particular users, the package of skills and competences itself is intrinsically neutral (Hannon 2000). This has been named the 'autonomous model of Literacy' (Street 1984). For many this position on literacy is 'common sense', but, of course, from an ideological perspective this is misguided and masks the underlying implications and power relations that lie beneath this unitary model of literacy. Here emerges one of the bitter fundamental disagreements between the left and the right in education politics. For particular factions on the left, informed by major theoreticians like Bourdieu (1991), the constitution of language is seen as a historical, political and socio-economic struggle between economic forces to exert linguistic domination over others, while those on the right condemn such views as nonsense, or even lunatic. It is important to say that not all left-leaning scholars and activists entirely agree with this sociological position and that pluralist views of literacy are often placed in the postmodernist and 're-constructed Marxist' accounts of educational theory and practice. I will discuss this in Chapters 2 and 4. Here I want to introduce pluralist ideas on the concept of literacy in readiness for later chapters.

In Gee's (2001) definition of literacy he links the term to the concept of discourse, which he describes in similar terms as I have above. He asks, 'How does one come by the discourse that he controls?' (p. 3). To answer this question he makes a useful distinction between 'acquisition' and 'learning' (Gee 2001, Krashen 1982, Krashen and Terrell 1983). By acquisition he means 'the process of acquiring something subconsciously by exposure to models and a process of trial and error, without a process of formal teaching' (Gee 2001:3). Acquisition occurs where the acquirer knows that what is acquired is meaningful and functional. This is how most people come to control their first language. On the other hand, for Gee: ' "learning" is a process that involves conscious knowledge gained through teaching' (2001:3) this may not always be from an official teacher in an institution of learning. 'This teaching involves explanation and analysis . . . attaining, along with the matter being taught, some degree of meta-knowledge about the matter' (2001:3). Gee's view is that one is better at things that are 'acquired', but one consciously *knows* more about what we 'learn'. He uses the activities of dancing, learning a second language or a musical instrument as examples of things one picks up through a mixture of learning and acquisition but, he argues, if acquisition is to predominate during that time one is generally better at them than if all exposure was through learning alone.

The idea of being taught to read in school through instruction would suggest that learning to read is achieved through 'learning' not 'acquisition'.

Yet this is said not to be true for all (Gee 2001, Street and Street 1991). As has been said, everyone is introduced to language through acquisition. The way we use language is socio-culturally determined (Heath 1983, Barton 1994, Gee 1996). Through a process of primary socialization within the family and community, we acquire what Gee (2001) calls the 'primary discourse' (p. 5), defined within the given culture. This is supported by Barton and Hamilton (1998) who have shown that literacy is not the same in all contexts, that these 'primary discourses' change from one social context to another. As Street and Street (1991) also contend: 'There are different literacies related to different social and cultural contexts rather than a single literacy that is the same everywhere' (p. 143).

Importantly, beyond these primary discourses there exist what Gee (2001) calls 'secondary discourses' that are utilized outside the family in various institutions – for example, schools, workplaces, universities, offices and churches. A secondary discourse is developed which can be more or less compatible with the primary discourses of other social groups. It becomes a great advantage to those wishing access to formal institutions that use a particular secondary discourse, if one's own primary discourse matches or is similar to that of the institution. The literacy in school is an example of a secondary discourse.

Street and Street (1991) explore how one form of secondary discourse or literacy has been formed and fashioned in schools, controlled by specific dominant cultural and class groups and conceptualized as the only form of literacy. It becomes the defining form – 'control of a secondary use of language used in a secondary discourse that can serve as a meta-discourse to critique the primary discourse' (Gee 2001:6). 'Street and Street' call the process in schools: the 'pedogogization of literacy' (1991:144). Literacy comes to be associated with what children learn in school at the expense of all the other forms found within alternative social contexts – other primary discourses. Street (1984) calls this the 'ideological model of literacy'. He goes on to say that school literacy curricula creates a divide between language and subject. A distance is created between 'language as a thing' and those who use it. This dominant secondary discourse critiques the primary discourses of other cultural contexts and potentially 'others' many of their users. However, for those familiar with this dominant use of literacy, this secondary discourse is a recognizable and decipherable cultural code that eases induction and development within this new environment. Gee (2001:7) comments:

Mainstream middle class children often look like they are learning literacy (of various sorts) in school. But, in fact, I believe much research shows they are acquiring these literacies through experiences in the home before and during school, as well as by the opportunities school gives them to practice what they are acquiring. (Wells 1985, 1986)

Those children who enter school from other cultural contexts, using primary discourses that are not compatible with the discourse or model of literacy used in schools, find themselves exposed to official language-use through a process of learning and not acquisition. They cannot practice in the school context what they have not found in their home cultures. It is here that patterns of underachievement in schools of children from particular social groups – for example, the working class – can begin to be explained.

This pluralist and ideological notion of literacy can be said to belong broadly to left educational discourse, but is contested by many on the right-wing of education (e.g., Honey 1997) and I shall be exploring some of these views in Chapters 3 and 6. However, I will also want to critique what the left offers as a means of countering and overcoming the effects of dominant discourses and what these measures mean politically for schools in capitalist economies.

In this introductory chapter, I have introduced readers to the key concepts that will form the foundation to the trajectory of the argument in this book. I began by offering a challenge to literacy educators to plot their position on the political landscape that shapes and informs policy and practice in the classroom. I have presented the problem that left educators are faced with in the consistence and resilience of patterns of underachieve-ment of working-class children. I have set out some of the main concepts and positions that I will draw on to analyse the answers educators offer as a means of improving the school chances of working-class children. I offered an introduction to the notion of a 'left and right' in politics. I have initiated an understanding of the concepts of ideology and discourse as key ideas in understanding educational motivations; provided a brief but essential history of education policy developments, pulling out the left and the right's meas-ures and motivations; and have begun to define literacy and the political tensions that make this area of the curriculum both frustrating and exciting.

The Organization of the Book

This book is divided into two main sections: the first provides a foundation of relevant political theory that will plot the political geography of the different approaches to teaching literacy. The two sections of the book are bridged by a chapter that explains how these political manifestations, described to that point, can be used to analyse approaches to literacy education. The second section presents the different approaches to literacy education within the context of wider political and philosophical contexts in order to analyse the aims and functions of these approaches.

In Chapter 1, the basic tenets of Marxism will be introduced and explored as classic 'left' transformative politics. The objectives of Marxism will be explained in a concise form along with Marxism's link to culture, literacy and education. This chapter provides an essential introduction to the 'father' of left politics and offers ideas that can be compared and contrasted with other left perspectives that have invested literacy teaching with its politics.

Chapter 2 will introduce conservative and social democratic liberal perspectives. In contrast to the last chapter, I explore the basic tenets of classic liberalism and neoliberalism from Adam Smith onwards. I will explain the objectives of this political perspective and introduce theorists and philosophers who advocate the unfettered power of the market. This perspective, too, is essential to understanding much of our present day literacy pedagogy. This chapter will also introduce social democratic liberalism and I will argue that in addition to its reformist objectives, it also has a conservative manifestation.

In Chapter 3, I discuss another, arguably, left-wing perspective – postmodernism and post-structuralism. Here postmodernism is discussed as an academic and political movement. The various positions of postmodernism are explained in a concise form, drawing on some of the main theorists and philosophers – including Baudrillard, Lyotard, Lather and Foucault. Its political manifestation is described and links will be made between political perspectives and literacy education.

Chapter 4 acts as a theoretical bridge between the politics and education of the book. In this chapter, I will construct a means of critiquing literacy pedagogies and approaches and identify their political and ideological root. Here I present my typology of literacy teaching based around the work of Bernstein (1996) and Bourne (2004). To set these 'left' approaches in a political context, conservative discourses will also be represented on this typology. The political left background of the forms of teaching will be examined from a reformist or revolutionary perspective, examining the social class assumptions of these perspectives and their 'Liberal', 'Critical' or 'Revolutionary' objectives that these positions advocate.

Chapter 5, 'Conservative Discourse and Literacy Practice' examines the literacy teaching associated with conservative neoliberal politics. Forms of pedagogy associated with this political stance will be explored. To do this, I will be concentrating on an analysis of the teaching of reading, with a particular emphasis on modern-day manifestations of the teaching of phonics.

Chapter 6 discusses social democratic liberal discourses and literacy practice. These approaches to literacy will include forms of 'romantic' and 'progressive' teaching with an 'invisible pedagogy' (Bernstein 2003). To do this, I discuss a specific example of practice from a professional development project that I was involved in. The project's aim was to change the nature of the pedagogy practiced in schools. These new practices, I argue, are forged from 'romantic' (Freire and Macedo 1987) perspectives of literacy teaching, and I use Bernstein's (1996) theoretical framework to explore arguments that conceptualize these pedagogies as being typical of social democratic left practices, and ultimately being conservative in nature. In addition, I analyse other contemporary literacy teaching, advocated by Mercer (2000) and others, which again, I argue, is less progressive than it at first appears.

In Chapter 7, I will explore the work and practice of those who advocate radical forms of pedagogy – including Friere – and their contemporary manifestations. These approaches will be conceptualized as being Neo-Marxist and aspire to transformative education within a capitalist economic context. These positions will be critiqued and analysed for their left-wing credibility and their potential for creating change in society.

Chapter 8, 'Marxist Discourse and Literacy Practice', examines what a Marxist revolutionary literacy pedagogy can be, drawing on classic Marxist theorists and revolutionaries, including Gramsci, Trotsky and Lenin. The educational function of a revolutionary party to promote class-consciousness will be raised as being fundamental to Marxist perspectives on literacy education for revolution. The problem of being a Marxist educator within a capitalist society will be explored and the argument examined that left literacy practice within a capitalist society may manifest itself in ways that may seem surprising to left-wing intellectuals and educators.

In the Conclusions, I offer some final remarks about education's potentially reformist or revolutionary nature. In this chapter, I will explore the argument that literacy pedagogy in its different forms is often a middle-class construction which is fundamentally 'conservative' in nature despite its 'left leaning' manifestations and political posturing. I argue that education has been used by social democratic liberal left politicians as a means to deflect demands for more radical political policies. This concluding chapter will summarize the analysis that has been made and questions the left credentials of much of the pedagogical theory produced by teachers and academics. Finally, I offer my own view of literacy on the left.

Part I

Political Theory

Chapter 1

Marxism: A Revolutionary Perspective

Why should someone interested in literacy education in the twenty-first century need to know about Marxism? Well, countless numbers of those who have wished to explore how to secure an equal society have been profoundly influenced by Marx's analysis of how humans have developed and the way the social order operates. His seminal works on social class domination and the materialist conception of history, in Marx's (1848) own words, created a 'spectre' that has haunted capitalism ever since the works were written. They also have implicitly constructed a penetrating and revelatory perspective on the role of education and, more specifically, on a school's approach to teaching about language and literacy. Debates about the conceptions of literacy and its uses have been consistently tied to the nature of power and the potential for resistance. The work of Marx sits at the extreme end of the left educational and political spectrum that I offer in this book and facilitates understanding of other forms of left politics which have influenced literacy education. It is my view that Marx's work cannot be ignored by anyone involved in education as practitioner, academic or parent. In addition, as we will see, his writings urge political self-analysis of one's role within education and as part of the state.

Having said this, despite writing a few short remarks and a few longer passages specifically about the subject, Marx did not write any whole works on education. His major concern was society in general, and any material on education was written within this context. Marx was keen not to contribute to the literature on utopian forms of socialism and, consequently, most of his comments about education are about schooling in the industrial capitalism of his time. Ideals were not his guide. Instead, he utilized an analysis of what was happening to society then (Small 2005). Furthermore, as Eagleton (1976) rightly reminds academics, Marx was a revolutionary and provided a scientific theory of human societies and how to transform them. There is nothing academic about revolutionary struggle. Yet, his work profoundly affected the ideas of many of the most famous educationalists:

Vygotsky, Voloshinov, Gramsci, Friere, Bernstein, the list goes on. Marx has also influenced the ideas of so-called 'Neo-Marxists' and postmodernists whom I discuss later in the book. Indeed, one might wish to argue that many of the ideals and aspirations of education practice, some of which can still be seen in classrooms in Britain and the United States, have been fashioned by those with at least an affinity with Marxism and their interpretation of how to use it.

In this chapter, I describe some of the basic tenets of Marxism. In doing so, I hope to provide readers with a clearer understanding of how Marxists analyse human development, culture and society. Of course, one has to recognize that Marx's work has been interpreted in various ways and bitter disputes continue to rage over the 'correct' Marxist perspective and how the ideas can be used for an analysis of schooling (Rikowski 1997). However, in this chapter I shall cover:

- the Marxist view of history and the development of capitalism;
- Marx's approach to understanding the workings of capitalism, the state and the fundamental importance of social class, 'labour power' and exploitation;
- Marxist interpretations of the relationship between the working class and art and literature.

I will then begin to examine how Marxism can heavily influence an approach to understanding the role of language in capitalist society. I will show how the ideas of Marx have influenced later writers in the field of linguistics and literacy education and the ways they have been interpreted by contemporary educationalists.

Historical Materialism

One of the most famous quotations from Marx concerns his conception of history and the development of human beings. He says: 'It is not the consciousness of men that determines their existence, but on the contrary, their social existence that determines their consciousness' (1859:263). Marx describes how social change and progress is determined by the nature of humans' social relations and the consciousness it brings forth. This is itself fashioned from what the organization and provision for production of the time can provide. In other words, the way people organize themselves to produce the means for their own subsistence is dependent on the forms of productive technology available to them and that these types of product-ive methods in turn dictate the nature of social organizations and the relations therein. Changes in the way production takes place produce new ways for humans to interact and thus create opportunities for shifts in cultural, intellectual, and political activity and consciousness – these shifts are manifested in revolutions. This is Marx's materialist conception of history.

The modes of production that history has shown human activity to have existed within – foraging, horticulture, slavery, feudalism and capitalism – have their own set of social rules and relations (D'Amato 2006). Marx shows that many of these modes of production had a ruling elite and an exploited class. Yet Marx and Engels also explain that this has only been the case for the last 10,000 years (Sewell 2007). For the rest of humanity's existence there was no class society and no forced inequalities. Different production relations produced a different form of social consciousness and society. Social progress, for Marx, was not governed by external ideas or a fixed state of human nature, but by 'the development of material production, which is the basis of social life, and therefore of real history' (Marx 1845). Slavery, feudalism and capitalist societies have been built on a system of oppression and exploitation, all of which, despite the cruelty and barbarity that they consequently created, were the driving factors for human development. Marx claims to study society scientifically. Despite the fact that Marx was aware of the injustices of capitalist society and had a vision of a fair and democratic world, he was not led primarily by a moral imperative.

The totality of the social organization of society is formed by the particu-lar mode of production existing at the time. The mode of production forms the 'base' of society. Marx describes this totality of social organization as the superstructure. Under capitalism (our present mode of production), wealth is measured not in land and slaves, like in previous productive relations, but in money. Capitalism's birth, around the developed world, occurred at the time of the industrial revolutions and as feudalism – a system based on the unpaid labour of peasants working on the land of the aristocracy and which could no longer sustain and utilize the technologies being invented and introduced – came to an end. The early success of feudalism also brought with it the seed of the system's demise. This was because the changes in population and the rise of a new moneyed class of merchants, bankers and factory owners – the middle class – were a part of feudalism's impact. The middle class later became the new ruling class of capitalism, replacing the lords and barons of feudalism.

According to Marx, each ruling class will initially act as a force for change and development, but as their rule progresses they begin to prevent any further progress or beneficial changes. Contradictions then arise between the *forces* of production (the means of production available), or the *base,* and the *relations* of production (the social organization of society) – the superstructure. These contradictions create epochs of revolutionary change and are evident in the growing tensions and antagonisms between the contending classes, resulting in revolutionary upheaval and a transformation of society.

> At a certain stage of development, the material productive forces of society come into conflict with the existing relations of production or – this merely expresses the same thing in legal terms – with the property relations within the framework of which they have operated hitherto. From forms of development of the productive forces these relations turn into their fetters. This begins an era of social revolution. (Marx 1859:263)

A Marxist analysis attempts to demonstrate that the move from feudalism to capitalism manifested itself in the revolutions that occurred in Europe and America in the seventeenth and eighteenth centuries – the English Revolution of the 1640s, the American Revolution of 1776 and the French revolutions of 1789–94. These were the struggles that were the foundations for the domination of capitalism on a world scale (Sewell 2007). What transpired then – and what Marxists believe will occur in the future, as capitalism is swept away by a workers' revolution – was that 'Molecular economic changes produced economic contradictions, which in turn produced social and political conflicts – class struggle – in which the old relations are overthrown and replaced by new ones' (D'Amato 2006:38).

Marx saw the overthrow of capitalism led by the working class as the means to the next stage of human development. Capitalism, like all the previous modes of production, will also become a fetter to the capacity for further development. It, too, by the nature of its base and superstructure, has contributed to its own destruction. Capitalism has created an exploited working class which is concentrated in large masses and empowered by their potential for collective action. Indeed, capitalism is based entirely on a form of social production. The global market binds everything into one economic unit, creating a network of multidependency. Furthermore, as history has shown, capitalism works within a system of booms and slumps. In the first decade of the twenty-first century, readers have witnessed further evidence of the recurrence of economic slumps and crises, which, Marxists contend, reveal an inherent weakness in the system and contribute to perpetual insecurity in the working class, which fears unemployment and, consequently, poverty. For Marxists, each new crisis demonstrates the need for the working class to change society. But only when capitalism can no longer offer workers hope of prosperity will they collectively, through the organs of the labour movement, carry out their historical mission to overthrow the system and create a classless society.

Marx demonstrated that socialism must have a material basis and could only manifest itself through the development of productive forces under capitalism. This is in contrast to so-called 'utopian socialists' who see the advent of socialism as a moral imperative rather than the next stage in human development. From this moral perspective, the role of education can be fundamental as a means of passing on these ideals courtesy of a radical and enlightened middle class teaching force (Woods 2008). Indeed, forms of literacy education have been seen as a means of resistance and fundamental change (Friere 1976). From this perspective, in order to prepare for revolution, education's role within the superstructure can be changed by those working from within. I shall discuss these ideas further in Chapter 7, in my analysis of critical literacy education perspectives. Marx insisted that the abolition of capitalism required the active participation of the working class at a specific stage in human history that was ripe for revolution. They will be forced, through economic crisis and hardship intrinsic to capitalism, to move society on. Indeed, Trotsky went so far as to declare that revolutions only occur when economic crisis compels the working class to deliberate over the choice between suicide and revolution.

The possibility of a classless society is what guided all of Marx's perspectives (Small 2005). He constructs the prospect of a society of the future with no class divisions, where all have equal responsibility in the processes of production and equal rights to the product. Socialist society is a return to the primitive communism discussed earlier, but on a vastly expanded productive level. The means of production would be usurped by the democratic control of the mass of the people. Capitalism has created the conditions for an organized and conscious working class to form a genuinely democratic society and to smash the state apparatus of capitalism.

Base and Superstructure, Education and the State

As we have seen, Marxism contends that we live in an epoch governed by a ruling class that owns the commanding heights of the economy. This class is made up of those who control business: the industrialists and the bankers. Together, they form the economic and political *base* of society – capitalism. It is these people who determine the way we live and, of course, how we are educated through the system of a *superstructure*. They do this through the organs of the state and through other components of the superstructure. The base brings the superstructure into being and gives it its character. The superstructure, with all its elements, in turn works to maintain the base and structure of society (D'Amato 2006). So, for Marx, the ruling class does not control just the material forces in society (the base) but is also its ruling intellectual force and controls the means of intellectual production (part of the superstructure). This class directs the state and, through its institutions, fashions our consciousness and outlook.

> The production of ideas, concepts and consciousness is first of all directly interwoven with the material intercourse of man, the language of real life. Conceiving, thinking, the spiritual intercourse of men, appear here as the direct efflux of men's material behaviour . . . we do not proceed from what men say, imagine, conceived, in order to arrive at corporeal man, rather we proceed from the really active man. (Marx 1845)

With this in mind, we can begin to understand how education fits into this doctrine and how literacy teaching is also part of the superstructure.

The structure and base of society is defended, mediated and administered by the state. Lenin uncompromisingly wrote that the state is 'a machine for the oppression of one class by another, a machine for holding in obedience to one class, other subordinated classes . . .' (1919:14). The state machine consists of the police, army, law courts, parliamentary parties and judges. As we will see, teachers, social workers and other state employees and institutions also have their role to play in this state machine (Althusser 1971). For Marxists, the state, with all its areas of interest and manipulation, is an instrument of class rule. It retains pretensions to provide a social unity, which is portrayed as being somehow neutral and unconnected to economic power, but this is simply a falsehood. The true function of the state is to reinforce and perpetuate the class power that already exists in society (Small 2005).

The state can manifest itself in different ways. It exists in both democratic and totalitarian societies as part of their superstructure because it stands above society. In times of political and economic stability, the ruling class have control of the state, but, as we have described, there are certain periods when the class struggle reaches such intensity that a question of power is posed for all. Either the revolutionary class overthrows the old, replacing it with a new power, or the ruling class crushes the revolting masses and imposes a dictatorship – state power in an undisguised form, as opposed to the state in democratic clothing (Woods 2008). Therefore, for Marxists, in any state, either democratic or other, the state is an instrument of repression.

Marx's legacy has been utilized by more contemporary writers specifically to critique modern education systems in advanced capitalist countries. Using Marx's analysis of class society, these scholars have developed academically influential work.

Althusser (1971), in discussing the state's control over individuals, also distinguished between the 'repressive state apparatus' (RSA) – the government, army, police, courts and prisons – and the 'ideological state apparatus' (ISA) – religion, education, family, trade unions, political parties, media and culture. RSA is utilized when the state deems it necessary to reveal its ability to use force to maintain and defend the existing order. The ISA, on the other hand, is the ruling class's preferred repressive apparatus and is described by Althusser (1971) as being a less unified collection of structures. These institutions – including education – support the ideology of the ruling class by imposing a set of values, abilities and traits that reinforce the divisions, attitudes and mores of capitalist society. For Althusser, schools have a central role to play in modern societies as part of the superstructure, having replaced the church's function to inculcate and compound the ruling class's ideology.

Books, art and culture, it has been argued (Plekhanov 1953), form part of the superstructure of society as a part of that society's ideology. To really understand this culture, its artefacts and how its mores are passed on, we must first understand the total social process within which it resides (Eagleton 1976).

The Grip of the Superstructure

The perspective, which holds that every society needs to maintain itself by reproducing in its new members the knowledge, values and habits that make them part of the social structures that exist in that society, was given further support by twentieth-century sociologists. In the 1970s, drawing on Parsons (1959) and Dreeben (1968), Bowles and Gintis (1976) wrote about schooling in capitalist America. Parsons (1959) had described how schools were places of socialization within which children are selected for their later roles in society. Success in school was measured by which role-models most attracted the children: their teachers or their peers. Those whose behaviour began to resemble the teachers had more chance of success (Small 2005). Dreeben (1968) later argued that children do not simply learn the content of the official curriculum but also a set of norms or principles of conduct. Bowles and Gintis (1976) added a class-based analysis to this critique of schooling. They formulated what they called a 'correspondence principle' which appeared to compliment Marx's view of a 'superstructure of society' imbued with the rules, values and regulations of a particular mode of production – in this case, capitalism. For Bowles and Gintis, there are systematic parallels between the features of the school and the workplace in a capitalist society:

> Specifically, the relationships of authority and control between the administrators and teachers and students and students and students and their work replicate the hierarchical division of labour, which dominates the work place. Power is organised along vertical lines of authority under administration to faculty to student body; students have a degree of control over their curriculum comparable to that of the worker over his job. (1976:12)

Bowles and Gintis (1976) argued that much of the organization and ethos of schools resembles the daily organization of workers in their place of employment. This included the emphasis in many schools on competition rather than cooperation that set up antagonism between students. In this view, even the timetabling was inculcated; it prepared students for an ordered working life, where conformity was met with praise.

Criticism of Bowles and Gintis's approach comes from those who argue that their position was overly deterministic (Apple 1985, 2004; Giroux 1983; Cole 1983) and left no room for individual agency and the possibility of spaces for resistance. (I will discuss this in more detail in my conclusion, where I discuss 'relative autonomy' theory in connection with literacy teaching.) Critics suggest that Bowles and Gintis create the impression that opposition to the superstructure is futile and, in effect, construct a position of hopelessness. Yet, accusations of economic determinism are also directed at Marx's materialist conception of history in general. Marxists (Sewell 2007, Woods 2008) (including Engels) have vigorously denied these accusations of a strict economic determinism. Marx wrote that people make their own history, but within the context of the present circumstances and those transmitted from the past.

As we have seen, Marx believed that in each stage of human development the productive forces of each epoch correspond to a specific set of productive relations (base and superstructure). These in turn provide the conditions of social existence. But this does not deny the presence of ideas and perspectives that run counter to the ruling ethos, or the possibility and necessity of making active contributions to affect change. After all, each economic epoch, each base of society, according to Marx, contains the seeds of its own destruction. These seeds are planted by the social conditions of the time and can be exploited by those aware of their historical significance. For Marxists, historical materialism has nothing in common with any form of fatalism. Humankind does not simply consist of puppets at the mercy of blind historical forces, but neither are we entirely free agents, operating irrespective of the existing social conditions. Marx himself wrote:

> Men make their own history, but they do not make it as they please; they do not make it under self-selected circumstances, but under circumstances existing already . . . the tradition of all dead generations weighs like an Alp on the brains of the living . . .

Bowles and Gintis's position, perceived using this analysis, can be viewed as a contribution to the Marxist science of perspectives (Sewell 2007) and as a further step towards understanding society in order to intervene within it. Yet, for Marx, a true change of society can only come about when the base of society has been fundamentally transformed. Superstructural changes, like changes to education, can only amount to tinkering on the peripheries of an economic system and cannot in themselves be deemed to be revolutionary. In many cases they may be classified only as reformism.

Social Class

In discussing the concept of social class, I want to examine its importance in terms of what I have introduced previously in this chapter: its influence on teacher – student interactions and perceptions of each other, its importance for the Marxist notion of 'labour power' and the curriculum and finally its connection to how literacy is conceived and taught.

As I mentioned earlier in this chapter, societies have not always been based on a system of exploitation by one class over another. For Marx, the earliest phase of human development consisted of a primitive form of communism in which there were no classes, private property or state. A class society emerged at the point when people were able to produce a surplus, more than the needs of the survival of the individual. It then became feasible for a division of society into classes to begin.

> On the broad scales of history, the emergence of class society was a revolutionary phenomenon, in that it freed a privileged section of the population – the ruling class – from the direct burden of labour, permitting it the necessary time to develop art, science and culture. Class society, despite its ruthless exploitation and inequality, was the road that human kind needed to travel if it was to build up the necessary material prerequisites for a future classless society. (Woods 2008:79)

With the exception of early primitive forms of communism, every society throughout history has been organized by some form of division of labour into classes who have unequal responsibilities and rights (Small 2005). Each class has a different function within the production processes of that society. This necessarily means that there is an imbalance of power and one class has access to advantages in rights and has power over the other classes. This state of affairs contributes to an inbuilt set of antagonisms which lead to irreconcilable differences between the classes. These differences form the seeds of that mode of production's later destruction.

For Marxists, the working class are conceived as those who have no means of production and as a consequence need to sell what Marx calls their 'labour power' in order to survive. All those who are forced to sell their labour – their capacity to work – are, for Marx, working class in a capitalist system of production and exchange. Marx shows how society under capitalism is divided into two classes – the working class and the ruling class.

In advanced capitalist countries, workers are now employed in a variety of jobs – in offices, in factories and in shops. Many, in what may be called the middle layers of society (the lower middle class), also make a living from a working wage. They may have benefited from longer periods of time in education and would have expectations of earning more financial capital and consequently also more social and cultural capital (Bourdieu 1986).

Social capital, as conceptualized by the sociologist Bourdieu, is the access one has to resources based on networks and membership to powerful social groups. It is 'who you know' that can lead to favour and advancement. Cultural capital is defined as one's own dispositions of the mind and the body and one's 'taste' in cultural activities. It also means the access and possession of cultural goods such as educational qualifications, which bring advancement.

Some forms of labour power, for example, professional labour power, and the range of capital it brings, arguably objectively and subjectively distinguishes the middle layers of society from those exponents of lower paid forms of labour power. I would want to include in this category of workers many employed in state and private education. Yet, increasingly there have been arguments to suggest that these professional layers of society have had their own working lives proletarianized over the last 30 years (Ozga 1988). Like other wage earners, they have had employers who are also concerned about cutting wages, and extending and intensifying the working day. In addition, the process of proletarianization has brought prescribed routines and a process of deskilling in a range of service sector organizations (Ainley 1993, Maguire 2001). This has been noted (Apple 2004) to be particularly true of schoolteachers and those across the education sector.

Labour Power

I want to look now at labour power, a concept that I touched on earlier. It concerns the subject of this book and its examination of left approaches to education and literacy and is directly related to Marx's position on class. For some modern Marxist educationalists (Rikowski 2000), labour power is the central concept for an analysis of the relationship between schooling and capitalism.

Under capitalism, the relationship between employer and worker seems one of exchange. The employer exchanges money for a day's work provided by the worker. Yet, Marx (CW) invites his readers to look to the underlying processes within this contract. He argues that in reality the worker does not sell the labour itself, but instead sells her mental and physical *capacity* to work. The value of this is determined by what it costs to keep the worker and her family alive and the price of whatever training or education has been necessary for the worker to undertake the job. This is labour power and the employer buys it as a commodity. The purpose of its purchase is to consume it by its conversion into actual labour. This work produces new and greater value. The quantity of this value is greater than what the worker receives from selling her capacity to work. *Part* of the days labour will maintain a *whole* day's labour power and so the value of labour power is considerably less than the value that labour power creates in the process of the work. The use of the labour power, a whole day's labour, belongs to him (the employer) even though it costs him only the equivalent of part of a day's labour' (Small 2005:77). The section of the product which goes to cover the worker's own subsistence and training Marx calls 'necessary product'; the part which the worker produces above this he calls 'surplus value'. This is the secret of the capitalist economy (Woods 2008). For Marx, capitalism needs to be understood, not from its exchange of labour-time equivalents but the appropriation of surplus value. As Trotsky (1963) has written:

> The class struggle is nothing else than the struggle for surplus product. He who owns surplus product is master of the situation – owns wealth, owns the state, has the key to the Church, to the courts, to the sciences and to the arts.

Literacy and Marx

I now intend to discuss questions that arise around the issues of literacy, which I introduced in the first chapter when using Marxism as a tool for analyses. I begin by an examination of pluralist conceptions of literacy from a Marxist standpoint. I then will explore how Marxism might be used to understand beliefs about the forms of literacy that need to be introduced to children – skills-focused or practice-based approaches – and finally literacy teaching's potential to change society by empowering the masses.

As I described in the 'Introduction', the pluralist view of literacy is based around the belief that literacy is always embedded in a culture. Since there are multiple cultures there must be multiple literacies. This will mean a variation in the particular written language and script being used within a given culture. It also will determine how this written language is utilized. Research (e.g., Barton 1994, Cook-Gumperz 1986) has attempted to show that literacy is a social practice and not a purely cognitive activity detached from any political context or set of social relationships.

School-acquired literacies have been provided with a definition that accrues them with neutrality from these contexts. This literacy contains an identifiable package of skills, which when acquired will ensure social access and success. Yet, ethnographic research (e.g., Hamilton et al. 1994) shows cross-cultural evidence that calls into question those who make claims for one homogenous literacy, one free from cultural influence. Any number of literacies have been seen to coexist within a range of social spaces, including the language use of children, different social and professional communities and classes. This has led to Street (1995) contending that literacy is more complex than current curriculum and assessment allow; that curricula and assessment that reduces literacy to a few simple and mechanistic skills, fails to do justice to the richness and complexity of literacy practices in people's lives. Street advocates curricula and assessment that are themselves rich and complex and based upon research into actual literacy practices. Yet, using a Marxist perspective this relativist and, arguably, postmodernist approach to culture and literacy (see Chapter 3) is problematic and questionable.

Working Class Culture

In order to explore a Marxist approach to this subject it is necessary to begin with a Marxist perspective of culture. To begin with, culture, according to one of William's (1983) definitions, is the way of life of a particular community or social grouping. With this in mind the working class, as defined by Marx, will have cohesive cultural traits that are linked to their position in society among the productive forces that define them as a class. Indeed, it is this collective class-consciousness and the physical proximity of their lives that are perceived as the seeds to capitalism's future demise. Marxists would contend that the working class has much in common in terms of their collective irreconcilable differences with the ruling class who consistently attempt to find the means to gain greater surplus value from their labour power. Furthermore, the working classes' reliance upon selling their labour power makes life fraught with the fear of unemployment, causing unease and potential unrest which consequently adds to their dissatisfaction with capitalism as a class and culture.

Modern sociological accounts (Dennis et al. 1956, Hoggart 1958, Young and Willmott 1957) have provided various descriptions of working-class cultures in the twentieth century. Often they have been positive, nostalgic and romantic in some of the descriptions they offer (Bennett et al. 2006). Working-class culture from these sources is typified by hard work, neighbourliness, cooperation and dignity. Other sociologists have argued that the cohesion of the working class has been diminishing (Offe 1985, Turner 1988, Pakulski and Waters 1996, Pahl 1993) due broadly to an *embourgeoisement* thesis that suggests that everyone is now middle class.

However, research by Goldthorpe and Marshall (1992) argues that the best available empirical evidence shows very little change between class and specific attitudes, mobility and education. As a consequence of similar incomes, similar pastimes and leisure pursuits common dispositions are generated. Bennett et al. (2006) demonstrated that the 'working class, when its boundaries are drawn with reference to cultural position and taste, is distinctive in aggregate' (p. 212). With this research in mind, links between literacy and cultural practices, as discussed in Introduction, become very relevant in terms of the working class and their literacy education.

Bourdieu's (1984) emphasis on social practices led him to formulate the notion of the habitus. *Habitus* is 'a Latin word that refers to a habitual or a typical condition, state or appearance, particularly of the body' (Jenkins 1992:74). Bourdieu's belief, based upon his own research was that a person's class classificatory dispositions are embodied within them. The habitus exists through and because of the practices and interactions with others. It is embodied through our ways of talking – our use of language and literacy; our ways of moving, our body shapes and all our behaviours enacted through our physical being. The body for Bourdieu is a mnemonic device (Jenkins 1992) within which our very culture is imprinted and encoded. For our purposes, how a person speaks is an important indicator of their social class. Language is part of the embodiment of working-class culture.

It is important, however, that Marxists do not favour or eulogize the cultural state of the working class under capitalism. Marxists would support the view that the cultural lifestyles of working class people should be respected and valued. Yet, Marxism would also argue that the cultures that have been developed within the working class have been generated because of the relations produced through the organization of production within a capitalist economy – the base and superstructure. The working class are an oppressed group and consequently have much of their lifestyles forced upon them due to economic circumstances. The existence of social class is intrinsic to the base of capitalist society and the working class and their culture are part of the superstructure of society. Marx argues that contradictions exist within capitalist society. In this instance, the working class form the cornerstone of the superstructure of its society, yet will eventually lead to its demise.

For Marxists, capitalism is one important stage in the development of human societies. The next stage – a classless society – brought about by a revolutionary period, led by the working class, would eradicate the state and the exploitation of one class by another. Marxism foresees an end to the relations of production that create a class society and the cultures therein, heralding a new epoch where all can engage in the riches of a human artistic and scientific development.

The nature of the new cultures produced through socialist change are unknown, but Marxism contends that such change should lead to universal access to the fruits of humanity's scientific and artistic potential through a genuinely thorough democratic politics. What is more certain principally for Marxists is that a 'working class culture' will never exist – not if what is meant by this term is a culture that belongs to the working class. Nor would it be desired. The culture that currently corresponds with groups of working class people under capitalism cannot be judged in a particularly favourable light by Marxists. It is simply the culture attributed to working class people under capitalism. In a sense, it belongs not to workers but to the ruling class of society. It will ultimately be swept away when the next phase of human development is brought about. A culture linked to the working class could only be positive in so far that it forms part of the seeds of capitalism's own destruction. It has no universal validity and it will perish.

Typically, Marxists do not attach any moral or romantic notion to the culture of working class people within the confines of capitalist productive processes with its consequent relations. The culture attributed by capitalism to the working class is a necessary transitory state of being in the development of human society. In actual fact, this culture does belong to the working class as they are a 'non-possessing' class.

The 'Nonpossessing Class'

Leon Trotsky, alongside Lenin, led the Russian Revolution and became one of the leading writers on Marxism in their epoch. In 1922 and 1923, he wrote about culture and post-revolutionary literature. He wanted to counter the arguments of some in his party who described post-revolutionary artistic work as a form of 'proletariat culture'. Trotsky argued that the period within which they were entering was only a lull in the progress of the revolution and the central objective had yet to be reached. The goal was the ultimate objective of Marxism, the creation of a classless society. So, their fundamental aim was to witness the demise of class in all its forms, including the working class. It is over this issue that Trotsky discusses the nature of working-class identity linked to culture:

The proletariat was, and remains, a nonpossessing class. This alone restricts it very much from acquiring those elements of bourgeois culture which have entered into the inventory of mankind forever . . . the

proletariat is forced to take power before it has appropriated the fundamental elements of bourgeois culture; it is forced to overthrow bourgeois
society by revolutionary violence for the very reason that society does not
allow it access to culture. (1980:47–50)

Trotsky wrote that the working class lacked the means of acquiring a culture
– a proletarian culture – and historically was destined never to have one. He
contended that 'by taking into its own hands the apparatus of culture – the
industries, schools, publications, press, theatres, etc. – which did not serve
it before . . . opens up the path of culture for itself' (Trotsky 1980:47) and
not just for the ruling class or even the working class. The society that
Trotsky wanted was one where the wonders of human culture (a 'culture for
itself') are freed from class control of any kind, as class society is destroyed
through revolution. Trotsky has been criticized (Foucault 1966) for what
has been seen as his bourgeois-influenced perspectives. He was said to
have an overly respectful attitude to the culture currently in the hands of
the ruling class. This suggests a universality of value. This runs counter to
post-structuralist accounts of culture. However, for Marxists, part of the
working class's subjective and objective condition is nonpossession.

Smashing Class Literacies

Where does this lead the notion of the need for equality within a plurality
of literacies existing within capitalist society; literacies constructed within
different class and cultural settings – a position advocated by many who
come from post-structuralist backgrounds and perspectives? For Marxists,
this is a reformist approach. Marxists have always supported efforts to
improve (Luxembourg 1970) the conditions of the oppressed members of
society, yet, ultimately, the issue is not a moral one, but is intrinsically related
to human development and the materialist conception of history.

The demise of capitalism and its replacement with a classless society would
herald the destruction of the cultures and cultural practices of those among
the oppressed class that have come into being through capitalist class relations. The fruits of human language development and its use lie within the
control of the ruling class. Along with artistic and scientific achievement,
access and control of rich literacy practices would be given to all in the
new society as a consequence of the transformation led by the working
class. It would also herald the opportunity for new, richer, complex cultural
advancement as a direct consequence of a new political and economic

epoch – a new base to society. In effect, this Marxist account attributes value to a unitary literacy – a powerful way with words, presently utilized and enjoyed by the ruling class and those with cultural capital – and promises its adoption, ownership and enrichment by everyone in the future. Literacy as a practice and pedagogy is part of the superstructure of capitalism. Like the rest of the superstructure, it works to maintain the power structures of society, by privileging the ruling class and oppressing the working class.

Unlike post-structuralist accounts of literacy practices and their attribution of equal worth and affordance, there is no belief in the importance of fostering them in working class children in capitalist schools. Marxists may argue that this post-structuralist approach is one associated with political perspectives that are resigned to the supremacy, longevity and resilience of capitalist society. There can be little allegiance to a materialist conception of history, and so they are forced to provide a moral and emotional critique of capitalist society with many of their answers to the vagaries of the market based upon reformism as opposed to revolution.

In Chapter 3, I will explore in more detail the postmodernist political perspectives that have led to post-structuralist accounts of culture and their subsequent literacies. These approaches are extremely influential in schools and universities as an alternative or 'New' left approach.

Literacy for Labour Power

> Times have changed, but the basic principle remains: capitalism needs workers who are clever enough to be profitable, but not wise enough to know what's really going on. (Wrigley 2006:2)

As covered earlier in this chapter, Marx describes how labour power is sold by working people to their employers to be turned into surplus value – the real profits of the ruling class. For Marx, labour power is a commodity and like all other commodities its value is determined by the labour time necessary for its production. Labour power is what the worker can do in a given industry or business. This makes schooling and training essential for the production of people with labour power of value in the given society. Rikowski (1992) describes how Marx (1867) depicted labour power as the aggregate of mental and physical capabilities and that consequently it becomes equated with what Rikowski (1992) calls 'personhood'. It is not just skills and physical capability that forms the essence of labour power, but also one's attitudes and dispositions.

Literacy and numeracy are two crucial components of this labour power. How a society conceptualizes literacy, and its manifestation in the curriculum, could arguably provide an indication of the kind of labour power required by most employers. Of course, one must concede that different employers have different ideas about what kind of labour power they want to buy (Wrigley 2006:2). Some will want a form of functional literacy – the labour power simply includes the ability to read and write and spell, while others will require labour power from their basic workers that has initiative and creativity as part of the deal. As we saw in 'Introduction', historically schools have been set up to produce more or less specific forms of labour power in their pupils. Arguably, the differentiation of children by ability into streams also differentiates between children's ability to acquire different labour powers to sell. In 'Introduction', I argued that after a relatively progressive period in the 1960s to the 1980s when teachers were using 'child-centred' methods in their teaching, drawing on children's own cultural interests to assist in curriculum formation (Jones 2003, Wrigley 2006), teachers in the United States and in Britain were faced with pressures to restore traditional practices. In the 1960s through the 1980s, English had begun to be taught in ways that drew on texts from a range of cultures and backgrounds, it began not to automatically privilege canonical texts and encouraged students to critically engage with the texts, interrogating them, using subjective insights to evaluate and produce multiple meanings.

In England, the introduction of the National Literacy Strategy (NLS) (DfEE 1998) provided further evidence that basic literacy practices were becoming the main objective for primary school teachers '. . . literacy emerged quickly and decisively as the key focus of formal education: the new bottom line' (Lankshear and Knobel 2003:7).

The NLS showed teachers 'how' to teach as well as 'what' to teach and greater structures of surveillance were introduced to ensure teachers' compliance with these methods. This included national testing and league tables and a threatening method of inspection. It has been argued (Johnston and Costello 2009) that many teachers find motivation for the methods they adopt through the fear of punishment rather than by professional alignment with what they are asked to do. What can also be seen from these changes is a radical reconceptualization of teachers' own labour power. Many of the skills, knowledge and dispositions thought worthy of teachers 20 years ago are no longer required as their own work has been proletarianized (Ozga 1988). This process involves the introduction of prescribed routines and a systematic 'deskilling'.

. . . teachers were well on their way to becoming a technical workforce to be managed and controlled rather than a profession to be respected. Those who argued that teachers should become reflexive practitioners, and that theory and practice in teaching should be inseparable, were presented by the radical right as enemies of good practice (Lawlor 1990). The nineteenth century view, that teachers should simply be trained to reproduce a set of technical operations and transmit subject knowledge . . . without a professional input, was resurrected. (Tomlinson 2005:41)

The literacy curriculum, took a turn in the 1990s that added fuel to the view that the history of literacy education shows, overall, its use as a means 'to solidify the social hierarchy, empower elites, and ensure that people lower on the hierarchy accept the values, norms and beliefs of the elites' (Gee 1996:36). As capitalism makes its globalization more explicit, the nation state needs to produce labour power that appeals to the ruling class and has needed to adjust its superstructure to cope. In doing so, education and training becomes reduced to the social production of labour power that can and wants to work for global monopolies. The right form of 'personhoods' (Rikowski 1992) can be developed by the production of particular kinds of labour power for ordinary people to sell and literacy education has the capacity to be fundamental in this process.

In this chapter, I have provided an introduction the ideas of Marxism that, since their inception, have been extraordinarily influential on the politics of the world. As I remarked earlier, any discussion of left politics needs to concede the place of Marxism. Indeed, Marxism in this book acts as the benchmark for all left approaches to politics and its influence on literacy education. Throughout the book, other forms of left politics and their manifestation in literacy education will be contrasted with those of Marxism. This chapter is of crucial importance for reading the rest of this book.

Chapter 2

Conservatives and Social Democratic Liberal Perspectives

While writing these opening chapters that describe the political perspectives that influence educational ideology and policy, I am aware that readers may be keen to arrive at explicit and uninterrupted discussion of literacy and literacy practices. The last chapter made some important links with Marxism and literacy, but I believe it is necessary to lay the foundations for discussion of literacy by introducing the relevant political positions and philosophies. Doing so will clarify for readers how and by what means literacy pedagogy is associated with an ideology and subsequent political policy. Giroux has written 'By recognising and interrogating the different layers of meaning and struggle that make up the terrain of schooling, radical educators can fashion not only the language of critique, but also a language of possibility' (1997:122). Marxism is said by its proponents to provide a scientific metanarrative with which many left approaches to analysing society and how to change it can be compared and, possibly, judged. Of course, within the left side of the political spectrum of educational and sociological theory, there is great complexity. Battles continue to rage about exactly how one would establish left-wing educational and literacy practices in school (Sayers 1979, Liston 1988, Rikowski 1997, Apple 1985, Mclaren 1987, Albright and Luke 2009). We will come to these later in the book, as it will be central to establishing what 'literacy on the left' can be. In this chapter, we must move further right of the spectrum to continue the analysis: to the advocates of liberal capitalism and the philosophical and political positions that now and in the past have influenced approaches to literacy and education practice in schools. With Marx acting as the foundation to left politics, what we conceptualize as 'conservative' must take on a broader canvas. For this reason, it becomes necessary to include in this chapter social democratic liberal perspectives, which broadly hold that a slow change to a more enlightened society and a more egalitarian education system is possible by reform of capitalism. The politically defining core of this perspective must be its commitment to the present economic base and its optimism about capitalism's potential for an altruistic impact on society. There is also a more right-wing angle to social democratic liberalism: aware of the dangers from a free market economy to the social order under capitalism, they seek to implement reforms that will quell any revolutionary fervour on behalf of the working class, offering concessions and forms of social mediation to address the plight of the working class. However, we must begin by examining the beliefs behind the global neoliberalization (Hill 2007) of education and the impact of this policy on literacy pedagogy and its conceptualization in the prescribed practice found in schools. Albright and Luke describe contemporary literacy education as being at a crossroads and at the advent of a resurgence of the policies of liberalism:

> If we are to take educational policymakers, politicians and the media at their word, it is the same great debate replayed over and over again: declining standards, loss of the literary canon, troubled by unruly students, irresponsible parents and overly permissive teachers. These, we are told yet again, can be fixed by marketization of schools, increased testing, a return to the basics of reading and writing. (2009:3)

This chapter begins with a brief description of classical liberal political perspectives that have fed and nourished this neoliberalism. In doing so, one must discuss the social democratic liberalism that historically is the reformist counter to market rule. Neoliberalism will then be discussed and analysed, followed by how literacy and literacy teaching is conceptualized from these powerful and influential perspectives.

Classical Liberalism

Classical liberalism was the political philosophy of early capitalism. Its roots lie in the English Revolution (1640–88) and the rise of the new middle classes who began to emerge from the ashes of the Stuart monarchy's imposition of absolute power and the demise of feudalism. Liberalism's traditions are not homogeneous (Jaggar 1983), but all have a unified and consistent approach to a belief in a specific form of human nature (Olssen et al. 2004). Liberalism is individualistic in nature. It asserts the primacy of the individual and is opposed to claims for the social collectivity of relations in society. Philosophically, liberalism contends that human nature is comprised of inner drives directed at the gratification of specific desires.

These innate compulsions are good because they are in harmony with the whole of society and humanity. The rights to inherited privilege, which had been the cornerstone of feudal society, were challenged by a belief in human nature's capacity for the possession of its own being and its propensity for reaching these desired ends by using rationality. The use of reason enables humankind to survive as it, although under no obligation to community or society, recognizes that peace and harmony would only come through some form of cooperation with others.

Hobbes, Locke, Hume and Bentham provided the philosophical and political justification for liberalism and its manifestation within British society. Although they did not agree on many of the elements of liberal philosophy in any form of totality, a central tenet in their thinking was a strong belief in 'self-ownership'. Each individual, they believed, was morally responsible for themselves and should make no claim to particular comradeship with others within a community. The state's role was to guide the individual freedom of each and every person, protecting their right to private property. Central to liberalism was the presence of constitutional government, but with a clear limit on the size and role of its remit. The safeguarding of the freedom of the individual had to be built into any system of government and the state should be bound by this limited mission.

Adam Smith, the leading economist of liberalism of the nineteenth century, was a strong believer in the market's capacity to counteract the necessity for a strong or invasive state. Up until the nineteenth century, the concept of natural rights of freedom justified protecting the individual from the state, but after this time liberal thought began to conceive of individual freedom from the state as being the best way to secure social good in terms of the 'greatest happiness for the greatest number' – as described most famously by John Stuart Mill (1859) (Olssen et al. 2004).

Liberal educational discourse portrays the developing human's potential to learn as something that is innate and supported by an individual's own efforts to succeed in the classroom. The child and, presumably, the parents are responsible for educational achievement. A human's natural drives and desires are the key to finding success at school and elsewhere. From a liberal perspective, social class, race and gender have little to do with the organization of the social world. They had no importance in the development of individual subjectivity or needs. However, there is an awareness built into this perspective that children need to be taught to respect their freedom and their capacity to be autonomous moral agents. Schools have a role to play here, but not at the expense of the state defining the criteria for a 'good' education (Gutmann 1987). Indeed, Mill famously warns that:

A general State education is a mere contrivance for moulding people to be exactly like one another . . . in proportion as it is efficient and successful, it establishes a despotism over the mind, leading by natural tendency to one over the body. ([1859]1972:175)

The basic tenets of classical liberalism have a twenty-first century manifestation in the contemporary neoliberal policies being implemented by Western governments – libertarianism, rationality, hierarchical authority, individualism, skills and personal efficiency provide the central thrust to this new political orthodoxy. All of which, I will argue in Chapter 5, provide the political and philosophical ghost within the pedagogical machine of contemporary 'conservative' prescribed literacy pedagogy.

Social Democratic Liberalism

Contemporary proponents of liberalism and neoliberalism (West 1994, Tooley 1996) insist that historical evidence about education before the intervention of the state in 1870 shows that it cannot be said that children of the nineteenth century were in need of state support. Most children, they insist, were in school, and literacy and numeracy rates were very high. In terms of literacy, West (1994) argues that the advent of new technology for the printing of newspapers had created a 'mass newspaper-reading public . . . already in existence well before 1870' (1994:158). Reading was a popular skill that had been learned in school. They argue that those who believe in state education have exaggerated the need for this form of intervention in schooling. Yet, as I have discussed in my short history of education policy in the introduction, the intervention of the state in schooling and in other issues of welfare was – in the face of revolutionary fervour in Europe and unrest in Britain – interpreted as intrinsically about the need to control the new urban working class. By so doing, this would also 'fit them' to serve the new industrial middle classes who needed labour. Social democratic liberalism provided the philosophical and political justification for intervention by the state.

Early proponents of capitalism, who venerated the market as the driver within society for development, strove to increase the rate of exploitation by repeated lengthening of the working day. Employers themselves, unchecked by outside agents, created the terms of workers' employment. Despite what Tooley (1996) and West (1994) argue, there is plenty of evidence to suggest that, as a result, the workers who lived in the larger cities faced the worst horrors of squalor imaginable (McCann 1977, Reeder 1977, Rubenstein 1969, Selleck 1968, Sturt 1970).

From the 1860s on, the state began to take action on matters concerning employment, health and education (Shonfield 1965). Governments around Europe started to intervene with the economy as it was plain to see that the market could not provide adequately for many of the basic needs of the new working class. Under the banner of individual rights, the proponents of a new social democratic liberalism wished to include constitutional rights to a decent standard of living.

Olssen el al. (2004) contends that:

> What Marx failed adequately to see was the extent to which forms of social change were possible within capitalism and the extent to which the working class could secure concessions through both industrial (trade union) organization as well as through the extension of the franchise. (p. 111)

However, Marxists (Brooks 2007) argue that the arbiters of capitalism realized these reforms were in the long-term interests of the ruling class as they were a means of maintaining a labour supply that was fit to work. Brooks argues that 'capitalism develops a form of state appropriate to its own rule' (2007:74). It can fashion states that utilize everything from parliamentary democracy to fascism, but ultimately all such states are made as a means of defending private property and the rule of capital, and they will do so at any cost. Most tellingly, it was Joseph Chamberlain who, in 1885, asked 'What ransom will property pay for the security it enjoys?' (cited in Saville, 1977 and Olssen et al. 2004). Arguably, the welfare state was a concession provided by 'property' as the best way to govern society and to protect the economic system. For Brooks (2007), capitalism's advocates and leaders are shortsighted and greedy, they tend to make workers struggle for every gain they win, through trade union and industrial action in the teeth of ruling class opposition. As we saw in Chapter 1, democracy has been conceptualized as the ideal form of capitalist rule as it provides the working class with a semblance of control and makes adjustments to their conditions easier to implement. However, Marxism says that capitalism, like all other economic bases in the past, contains the seeds of its own downfall. The working class organizations that need to struggle to gain reforms and concessions from capitalist governments also become the most favourable means to overthrow their oppressors. Therefore, provided the funds are available, reforms can put back a revolution, yet they also are inherent in the means by which capitalism will eventually fall. To take away these reforms in periods of economic slump inevitably compels those workers in most need of the reforms to rekindle the irreconcilable differences between themselves and their employers.

Reform was seen by nineteenth-century social democratic liberals as an urgent necessity (Selleck 1968). Education in particular was perceived as vital to reducing crime and to providing the skills necessary to prepare the working class for the exercise of their new voting rights (significantly increased in 1884). Education was also crucial in helping to secure social order.

The 'socialist' Fabians were highly influential and helped guide much of the reforming legislation through Parliament. Building upon liberalism's belief in the autonomy of the individual, the proponents of social democratic liberalism proclaimed a belief in each individual's moral worth and intrinsic value, and it was these values that they believed must be reflected in the dignity that the individual should be allowed to accrue (Jaggar 1983). Yet, as we have seen, this moral perspective and belief in the need for all to cooperate was within the context of a strong, rich new capitalist economy, which needed to accommodate and prepare for the new class divisions that had been constructed during the industrial revolution. This vein of 'socialist' reformism was given its biggest test after the Second World War when, as Marxists (Grant 2002) contend, the time was ripe for genuine democratic socialist transformation. Yet the reformist Labour Movement looked into the abyss at the potential end of capitalism and, bolstered by the huge funds from the United States and the support of the Stalinist Communist Party and other reformist organizations around Europe drew back (see Chapter 1) and the support of other reformist organizations around Europe and the Stalinist Communist Party.

Liberalisms and Literacy

As Lankshear and Knobel point out:

> Given the benefits of . . . historically informed hindsight, it makes good sense to begin from the assumption that compulsory mass schooling probably has a lot less to do with *educating* and *making literate* (in any truly expansive sense of these terms) than it has to do with producing other outcomes; outcomes which we should strive to make clear, and for which we should call governments, education officials and teacher educators to account. (2002: 268)

These outcomes that Lankshear and Knobel raise must be the more instrumentalist objectives of literacy teaching. Conservative educational practice will often perceive culture and knowledge as being a part of a storehouse of artefacts that are conceived as a canon. As we have seen, classic liberalism portrays all learners as having the same inherent qualities of human nature. Given this perspective, a form of knowledge as cultural currency needs to be provided for children. This form of knowledge must be dispensed to the learners while ignoring the learners' differences or variety of interests. This view contends that prescribed shots of knowledge can 'inoculate' the learner from future threats of unemployment, poverty and the consequent moral depravity that can follow. This form of hypodermic knowledge has been called 'positive knowledge' (Cusick 1983, Giroux 1997). It is a knowledge which is generally accepted as having an empirical and traditional base. It is predetermined and hierarchically arranged, and given a learner's natural desire to achieve in life and society, it should be gratefully received.

Contemporary policy for literacy education could be interpreted as a reflection of this liberal perspective on knowledge. In England, Wales, New Zealand, Australia and the United States there have been moves to increase standardized testing and performance monitoring. Interactions between students and teachers have become centrally circumscribed. As an example of this, governments have been using legislation to ensure single methods for the teaching of reading are implemented in all state schools. Here, state intervention is used to ensure that all children have access to these forms of 'positive knowledge'. It can be argued that this policy takes a neoliberal approach, and I will discuss it in detail in Chapter 6. This form of liberalism offers a slightly revised role for the state, facilitating the means of addressing the needs of the market.

On the other hand, social democratic liberal educational and literacy practice has long been associated with what has been called 'progressive education' (Giroux 1997). It has developed relatively 'left' credentials over the years in terms of its radical contrast to more traditional modes of literacy pedagogy. Many progressive educators even borrowed from Marxist and Neo-Marxist pedagogues and educational theorists like Friere and Gramsci. Child-centred approaches associated with progressive education take into account the needs and cultural experiences of the children as a start for developing relevant forms of pedagogy. These approaches aim to build supportive links between language communities and, through reciprocal relations, between the community and the socio-culturally aware teachers. Together, they can negotiate a path through a curriculum. This collaboration enables the children to have access to powerful cultural capital and thus achieve in society.

There have, however, been significant critiques of this social democratic approach which aims to embrace community language and practices and to make compromises between school, curricula and local linguistic practices. Graff (1979), for example, describes this approach as 'buying in' to the 'literacy myth'. Graff shows how eighteenth- and nineteenth-century school reformers made direct links between the moral power of literacy and the amelioration of poverty and hardship (Luke 2009). Graff argues that this perspective has informed twentieth-century social democratic liberal views that literacy can be the driver to social and economic prosperity. Graff (1979) and others (Carrington and Luke 1997, Luke 2009), using Bourdieu's 'field theory' (1984, 1986, 1991) as an analytical framework, contend that although literacy matters, it cannot of itself always have these effects. As Carrington and Luke (1997) point out:

> . . . we still lack a capacity to model and predict the social effects of literate practices and discursive resources for individual and group life trajectories as they cross dynamic institutions and/or disciplines, that is the effect on people's lives as they move beyond the locality of the schools and home communities into increasingly diverse social fields. (p. 99)

Carrington and Luke (1997) describe how Bourdieu (1986) showed that literacy practice forms a 'powerfully mediating moment' (p. 100) among the web of regulatory social relationships that form social fields. These are the 'structured social spaces that are characterized by discourse and social activity' (Luke and Carrington 1997:100). Schools are just one among a number of social spaces that children will encounter as they grow up. Linguistic capital that is valued within one social space may not be valued within another. Luke and Carrington conclude that 'there can be no universally valued form of linguistic competence of capital, regardless of the claims made on behalf of school literacy by curriculum developers, teachers and others' (1997:101).

Giroux (1997) also criticizes these social democratic liberal views on education. He writes:

> In its most common-sense form, liberal educational theory favours a notion of experience that is equated either with "fulfilling the needs of kids" or with developing cordial relations with students so as to be able to maintain order and control in school. (p. 127)

For Giroux social democratic liberalism operates within an 'ideology of deprivation' (1997:127) in which educators believe that children from certain backgrounds have a deficit of culturally specific experiences that they must go on to acquire. According to Giroux, these educators fail to recognize that what is legitimized as a privileged school experience is an endorsement of a particular way of life, signified as superior by this ideological approach to schooling. I will continue with this critique of social democratic liberal perspectives more thoroughly in Chapter 6.

Neoliberalism

From 1979, when Margaret Thatcher's Conservative government was elected, a political resurgence of a classical liberalism that had been remixed for the twentieth and twenty-first century took hold during the dominance of the New Right, which Thatcher led. This new form of classical liberalism was, arguably, continued by Tony Blair and his predecessors (Ball 2008). A counterreform of welfare provisions had been in operation since the 1970s in countries that had been wealthy enough to offer social protections to those in the labour market and for those unable to work, and provision for universal education (Tomlinson 2005).To make savings within a capitalist economy that functions in a series of booms and slumps, and which had waved farewell to the golden age of capitalism in the 1950s (Hobsbawm 1994), the policy makers of the New Right were required to 'roll back the state' and to reinvent a form of Victorian laissez-faire individualism (Ball 2008). Back came assertions of the freedom to choose, individual liberty, market freedom and the disciplines of competition. Ball (2008) cites Thatcher's first conference speech, which sums up this neoliberal resurgence:

> Let me give you my vision: a man's right to work as he will, to spend what he earns, to own property, to have the state as servant and not as master: these are the British inheritance.

Yet despite the personalities and theories that pronounced and professed about the affordances of neoliberalism in contrast to those of social democratic liberalism and its economic and social policies, it is important to bear in mind that these two positions are simply the 'left and the right boot of capitalism' (Woods 2008:220). For Marxists, the return to neoliberal policies is purely the expression of a crisis in capitalism and a way of removing the poison of inflation from the system. Marxists contend that there are always objective reasons for each approach to managing capitalism. In reconstituting conservative liberalism:

> They have created a whole new language ('downsizing', 'liberalisation of capitalism', 'opening up of markets', 'freeing the economy', etc.) to cover up for what is really a massive destruction of productive forces and jobs. (Woods 2008:220)

In describing neoliberal perspectives I want to present a number of thematic headings that I intend to show have significant correspondence later on in the book with conservative methods of teaching literacy. I argue that it is no accident that this is so, as education and the teaching of literacy will inevitably be drawing on the same elements of one management system. These are: efficiency, skills, individualism, competition, hierarchies, rationality and libertarianism.

Efficiency

In classical liberalism, the state is seen as a negative force of power opposing the individual's need to be free to pursue their own drives for betterment. However, neoliberalism conceives the state as a means to providing the conditions, laws and institutions needed for the effective organization of society. In this vision, the state is used to make individuals enterprising, competitive, and proficient.

The neoliberal agenda rejects state welfare as it is seen as being highly inefficient. Competition is perceived to be a better way of guiding the individual efforts of people than any other method (Hayek 1944). An efficient system of production and distribution is one that is based on reciprocal relations. Like can be exchanged for like and all are satisfied. Fives uses an analogy to illustrate how the mechanisms of neoliberal capitalism operates.

> I may prefer to drink a glass of vintage wine every evening, and wine sellers may want £100 for such a bottle. I can only satisfy my preference, therefore, if I can also provide services or goods that others want and for which they are willing to pay me sufficient money to finance my wine-drinking habit . . . I am made better off (by receiving the wine) without making any one else worse off (no one is forced to subsidize my taste for wine). (2008:197)

Welfare, for neoliberals is inefficient, as it makes those who are disadvantaged and need welfare, better off, and by so doing makes the more advantaged worse off (Fives 2008). The distribution of wealth and goods to those who offer nothing in return encourages those same people to demand more for nothing (Plant 1991). However, for some proponents of neoliberalism (Gordon 1991), in a time that has seen universal welfare and its subsequent vagaries, knowledge of the capacity for slothful indolence makes vigilance, surveillance, performance and appraisal all the more necessary in a neoliberal world.

The implications of this perspective on the inefficiency of policies that use welfare include the selling of state-owned enterprises, goods and services to private investors. These include banks, railways, power services and schools (Cole 2009). Moreover, the cutting of public expenditure on social services like education and health, where these forms of welfare remain, would increase the levels of efficiency in the economy. The means need to be found to cut costs and offer services that are perceived to be the most efficient at meeting the objectives that these individual services can offer.

Shannon (2000, 2001) argues that this spirit of efficiency and the need to produce the most effective and tangibly useful product has been factored over into literacy education. It has become the main driver affecting most classroom literacy practice in the United States. He states that the efficiency movement in reading instruction began in the early twentieth century. Curriculum was a set of testable skills with speed and accuracy as the primary criteria for success. Accordingly, modern institutions, social norms, and even individual actions are developed and judged according to uncaring scientific and meritocratic business principles in order that they can be entered safely as factors into the calculus of modern life (Shannon, 2001). I will say more on this in Chapter 5 with my discussion of the teaching of phonics for learning to read. In the second half of this book, I will explore pedagogy for literacy that I will position on the right of the political spectrum, partly through its adherence and dedication to these forms of efficiency measures prescribed within schools.

Skills, Competition, Passivity and Human Capital Theory

Human Capital Theory (Schultz 1960, Denison 1962, Becker 1964, 1976) is central to an understanding of the principles behind neoliberalism and schooling. It renewed the concern for investment in education as the major factor that helps secure economic growth. Becker's (1976) position was that people can be induced to make competition central to how they perceive their lives being improved. By making education and schooling a sound investment in terms of what they can offer in skills and training for work, all rational people will choose schooling and the forms of 'positive knowledge' they offer to help guarantee their success in the market. For Human Capital Theory, workforce and management skills are the central ingredient to a prosperous national economy. It follows that most further and higher education will be targeted for the labour market and that all previous schooling will be concerned with the skills and knowledge required to reach this level of training or education.

Human Capital Theory advocates the generation of a 'training culture' (Fitzsimmons and Peters 1994) among those in society. Since the 1980s this theory has influenced those who wish schools to be active in developing a skilled and adaptable workforce to be able to compete on a world scale. Skill becomes the basis of all value and creates a prospect of infinite re-skilling (Olssen et al. 2004). For Olssen et al.:

> Human Capital Theory represents human beings as the passive playthings of external forces who will 'deteriorate' if not kept in good shape through rigorous training programmes . . . for Human Capital Theory, the sum purpose of human existence is reduced to the skill level or performance capacity of the population. (2004:150)

I want to argue later in this book that Human Capital Theory is at the core of the drives to change literacy teaching to be efficient and 'cost effective' in the United Kindom and other advanced Western nations. Part of the remit of the Independent Review of Early Reading, known as the Rose Review (DfES 2006) in England was to evaluate 'the value for money or cost effectiveness of the range of approaches' (p. 7). This perspective contributes to evidence of a discursive shift from social democratic liberal and progressive visions of teaching being an art, informed by intuition and sensitivity, to a vision of literacy teaching being about 'best practice' (Soler and Openshaw 2007). This shift of the pedagogic gaze led to a change in policy that emphasized efficiency (Labour Party, 1997) over all other considerations. A single method of the teaching of reading, provided by the harbingers of synthetic phonics, provides what contemporary governments perceive as rational and positivistic approaches to the teaching of reading – a 'positive knowledge' – and the skills that will produce the human capital needed for a buoyant economy.

The introduction of a clear, single model for the teaching of early reading, that Rose generally advocates and that subsequent policy has embedded in documentation and policy, sets up a transparent task for schools that forms part of a clear contract and mission that state primary schools have been tasked to achieve. This, I would argue, is symptomatic of a theory of work relations, intrinsic to neoliberal politics, known as agency theory (Olssen et al. 2004). This theoretical orientation to work relations conceives a contract constructed between the commanding principal and the agents tasked with a specific goal. Instead of a broad job specification based on an increasingly lost notion of professional autonomy and responsibility, it introduces a series of contracts between a commissioning principal who delegates work to an agent to perform in return for a specified punishment or reward. In the case of schools as agents producing certain forms of literate child, the task is clear and the performance indicators and designated punishments understood by all parties. This contract depends on clear and detailed objectives based around a hierarchically organized set of skills and knowledge which is in place for schools teaching reading.

I offer the connections between neoliberal theory and policy with literacy teaching as merely a taste of the discussions further ahead in the book. In this chapter, I have provided a brief description and analysis of liberal capitalism, its 'left and right' configurations in the form of classical liberalism and social democratic liberalism, and the contemporary re-emergence of ideas from the beginning of the capitalist epoch in the form of neoliberalism. I have not offered a thorough critique and analysis of these positions, but I hope to have provided enough background for readers to begin to grasp the basic politics and theory to what can be seen in society today and in the past. As I said earlier in this chapter, understanding the politics should help place literacy pedagogy in its various positions on the spectrum of political beliefs that drive its objectives.

In the next chapter, I introduce the extremely influential ideas of postmodernism and begin to make connections between these complex ideas and those of literacy teaching on the left and the right.

Chapter 3

Postmodernist Perspectives

In this chapter, we roll back over to the left of the political spectrum that these early chapters of this book have been analysing. It is here I want to examine some of the origins and foundations of educational thought and practice in the field of literacy that have been influenced by postmodernism. Its claim to revolutionary or left credentials seems to originate from the way postmodern thought has attempted to demolish Western intellectual orthodoxies through a wholesale attack on the central organizing principles of Western thought. Postmodernism attacks the logic of the grand narrative or metanarrative. Ironically, in so doing, it philosophically denies the very grand narrative that has been central to left politics: Marxism itself. Consequently, bitter disputes rage between Marxists and postmodernists in contemporary academic circles, the substance of which I have already begun to touch on in previous chapters. As I will show, instead of conceiving the proponents of postmodernism as fellow lefts, many Marxists view them as being fundamentally reactionary in outlook, condemning society as being unable to structurally change and effectively making left politics an anachronism (Cole et al. 2001). In discussing postmodernists' left credentials, as reflected in many of their proponents' writings, McLaren observes: 'Their revolution is basically an aesthetic one, and their revolutionary activity consists largely in going shopping' (2001:36).

In this chapter, I shall introduce some of the thought that has been called postmodernist and post-structuralist. I shall go on to discuss the alleged left politics that emerge from this philosophy and then shall describe how postmodernism has influenced education and, in particular, literacy teaching. I want to explore theories about literacy practices that extol the importance of resistance and change within local contexts rather than literacy that can change the world on the kind of global and totalizing scale that Marxist left ideas advocate.

Modernity and Postmodernism

'Modernity' is a state of being in a specific period of history and 'modernism' refers to social, cultural, aesthetic and political movements during that period (Cole 2008). Modernity is thought to have begun at the dawn of the modern industrial age and the end of feudalism. It came with the rise of capitalism, when the nation state was on the ascendancy and the new middle classes could afford to embrace the ideas of the enlightenment that heralded modernism. This meant that the demand for new technology and engineering would see the championing of rationality and science in preference to superstition and belief in a God. A new ruling class would mean fresh perspectives, huge advances in society and the liberation of ideas and perspectives that had hitherto been suppressed within feudalism. Marxism is a product of modernity. Its belief in progress and the evolution of societies is linked to the modernity of Darwin and his scientific perspective of the development of species.

Modernism is an acceptance of the ideals of modernity and what post-modernists were later to call the 'canonization' of these perspectives that were enshrined in the grand narratives that were released at the time. Modernism achieved official status in the schools, universities and politics of the modern world and built the metanarrative or the grand narrative that explained phenomena and processes as forms of truth. Modernism presents an authority that is based on a claim to authenticity and truth found by the use of reason. As we shall see, scepticism towards modernism came as a reaction

> to the over-confident certainties of an earlier age. A 'heroic model' of inquiry, particularly in the sciences, had prevailed since the eighteenth century, according to which the scholar was engaged in a dis-interested value-free pursuit of truth, conquering ignorance and superstition, and always in the service of human progress. (Bailey 2001:162)

Postmodernism presents itself as a resistance to modernism's certainty and resolution. It rejects fixed notions of reality. It wants to deliberately unsettle assumptions and presuppositions and will not accept boundaries or hierarchies. Things will no longer be either/or, but instead processes are complex, opaque and plural (Atkinson 2002). Postmodernism resists totality and closure of any kind. It distrusts the notion of origins – the first cause or foundation to which all subsequent assertions and claims to truth are formed (Sheehan 2004). Knowledge, then, is questionable and it is no longer the role of the traditional institutions to attempt to claim it.

Postmodernism is a term that crosses into various discourses. It moves through the realms of art, politics and into areas of, for example, film, television, fashion magazines and pop music. In all these examples, established knowledge of how to work within these disciplines is questioned. Indeed the discipline itself is challenged, through an interrogation of its claim of belonging to an individual activity with accepted boundaries and some form of static defining foundation at its heart. Knowledge is never linked to some external reality, as modernism wished to declare. Knowledge is instead open to question and suspicion, challenge and discussion.

Post-structuralism

In one form, post-structuralism is concerned with language. In its call for the deconstruction of certainties formed from language, it is the sister and theoretical base of much of postmodernism. Language understood in broad terms takes in all signifying systems, including images and symbols. It is these signifiers that give us access to information (Belsey 2002). When one acquires new knowledge, one also acquires a new vocabulary and syntax. Post-structuralists argue that with this language comes an introduction to the social values of the culture, which is based upon certain forms of linguistic use and literacy. Language carries meanings about the cultures, societies and the world within which we exist. This is called 'discourse'. Language comes packaged with meaning. As we learn the language and its uses, the meanings we receive are not ours to command, instead we become controlled by them (Belsey 2002). For post-structuralists, consciousness itself is not the origin of the language we speak, in fact, consciousness is the product of the meanings we learn to reproduce by our acquisition of language. We are given the meanings about the world through the language we receive from our culture – the discourse. Language's reference to the world is put into doubt. Yet, language is the prime mediator between humans and our world, it names and classifies the soup of sensations we experience and provides the meanings for them that the culture has embedded in the language.

It is language that provides us with the means to name the experiences we have and, by so doing, provides us with the means to distinguish between them. Post-structuralism generally asserts that these distinctions are not given directly to us by an objective reality, but are instead gifted to us by the symbolizing systems we learn to utilize.

The Swiss linguist Ferdinand de Saussure (1916) proposed that meaning does not depend on reference to the world or to ideas. Traditionally, words were thought to be signs. These signs were thought to represent something that existed in the real world. Nevertheless, Saussure asserted that the meaning only resided in the sign. He theoretically divided the sign in two parts: the signifier, which is the sound or visual appearance of a word, sentence, phrase or image; and the signified, which is its meaning. Saussure made the point that neither signifier nor the signified determines the other. The signifier does not by itself express the meaning, which is provided by the culture that uses it as a signifier, while the signified does not resemble the form or the sound with which it is connected. The word 'bird', for example, does not resemble in any way the object it is supposed to signify. Other languages use other words to represent a bird and these words have no resemblance to a bird either. Even the image of a bird, it can be argued, does not resemble a bird in real life. A painting is constructed from pigment and oil. Yet, over time, cultures have come to recognize the brush markings and use of paint as representing objects in the world. Meaning is differential, not referential, and this by itself has important implications concerning the relations between different sets of people around the world. People in cultures learn to recognize and use the signifiers as meaning-making devices.

The repercussions of Saussure's ideas have been huge as they strike at the very heart of what humanity has used to order knowledge, morality and society – language. Meaning, Saussure proposed, depends on difference and not reference. Meanings are ideological and cultural and are not based on a single reality. Indeed, reality of all kinds takes on a pluralist perspective relative to ideology, culture and subjectivity. Saussure's work and the later writings of French cultural theorists led to the highlighting of the unstable patterns of linguistic and, consequently, subjective social order. Jacques Derrida (1976) took up the mantle of this earlier work, interpreting the meaning of signifiers as being in a state of continuous flux. His position was that when a linguistic or social order is said to be fixed and stable, then this stability is based less on any truth and more on power and the ability of one group to impose its will on another (Cole 2008).

The world cannot exist as a thing-in-itself, something which is independent of human interpretation. It is a product of social practices – importantly, language practices – of particular communities and interpreters. The world as we think we know it is mediated, filtered and shaped by language that is passed on from culture and community through discourse. A statement about the world is conditioned by the specific context within which that statement is made. Truth is not universal, but rather 'multiple, historical, contextual, contingent, political and bound up in power relations' (St Pierre 2000:23).

Post-structuralism and postmodernism has inevitably led educators to question many of the orthodoxies of their own field. Postmodernist scholars have drawn on these perspectives to question seemingly embedded notions like, for example, the concepts of 'children' and 'childhood' from an ideological and cultural perspective (James and Prout 1997, Buckingham 2000). Postmodernism must also demand that the notion of literacy can no longer be conceived as something necessarily singular in its definition. This leads literacy to be conceptualized as ideological in character, bound to cultural contexts and, therefore, plural in its manifestation (Street 1984). This position in itself, which was discussed in the first and second chapters, has had an enormous impact on literacy theory and practice and has repositioned left thinkers on how literacy can lead to resistance.

Foucault's Power and Pluralism

Michael Foucault is primarily associated with the concept of post-structuralism and his work was directed at Marxism's deep theoretical structure. Foucault's post-structuralism worked against the Marxist idea that the economy and the base of society provided the determining source of explanation for the superstructure and was the organizing principle of the cultural formation in society.

> Rather than seek to explain all phenomena in relation to a single centre, Foucault is interested rather to advance a polymorphous conception of determination in order to reveal the play of dependencies in the social and historical process. (Olssen and Peters 2007:156–57)

Foucault advocates pluralism in place of what he saw as Marxist monism. He did not believe that there was one set of factors that directed the destiny of humanity as Marx did in his materialist conception of history (see Chapter 1). This perspective argues that Marxism makes the mistake, as other products of the enlightenment and modernity, of sourcing domination and power to a totalizing concept – capitalism. Foucault's perception of power had no one central source, but instead observed a number of power/discourse formulations as responsible.

> Power is everywhere . . . power is not an institution, nor a structure, nor a possession. It is a name we give to a complex strategic situation in a particular society. (1980:142)

For Foucault, Marxism has assumed a binary structure of power relations within society, where the dominators face the dominated in a society determined by these two powers. Instead, he believed in a multiform production of relations in the field of domination (Foucault 1980). Instead of struggle being totalized into a single cause, Foucault saw resistance and political action as being essentially local, diffuse and strategic.

Foucault perceived all relations between persons as being relations of power. In effect where there is hierarchy of any form – for example between adult and child, mentor and mentee – there is always an exertion of power. Any form of transmission of knowledge involves a form of instruction and therefore entails a form of submission. Power, and submission to it, is everywhere; it has no totality of source. The norms of society are culturally produced and by their exertion of a discipline, they form a type of oppression. For Foucault, a 'truth' exerted cannot exist outside of power, domination and submission. It follows that Marxism, thought by many as providing the theoretical basis to liberation, instead, by the very nature of its totalizing perspective, attempts to dominate and exert power, effectively oppressing alternative narratives.

Foucault celebrates singular events of resistance – by definition there can be no power without resistance (Belsey 2002). Unlike Marxism, he does not look to the grand moments in history that seek origins and sources of resistance to power. Instead, to understand the possibilities and the limits to resistance, Foucault looks to singular events and people who have been neglected by the grand narratives of history and politics.

Marxists argue that from Foucault's perspective, since there is no one source of central power, mass revolutionary activity is redundant and paralysed (Cole 2008). Indeed, followers of Foucault make no bones about it:

> For Foucault, the revolution as Marxism conceived it . . . fails theoretically to be plausible in a global age because it can only be taken seriously within a uni-linear and utopian frame of reference. What must be asked anew is how would such an idea of revolution be conceived, planned for, and organised in an age that is both global and local. . . . Indeed, to envisage a total sudden reconstruction or rendering of society . . . in advanced industrial nations boggles the mind. Hence, for Foucault . . . the drive for change must take the form of resistance and struggle in specific sites, utilising complex technologies and intellectual tools. (Olssen and Peters 2007:169)

As I will show, Foucault's ideas have touched the 'left' literacy theorists and educationalists in the perspective of how literacy can act as a form of resistance and liberation, concentrating on diffuse and local forms of action and practice instead of utilizing literacy education for the revolutionary ferment for later mass action.

Anti-Capitalism

Modern Marxist revolutionaries (Woods 2008) would condemn postmodern perspectives like the ones discussed above as being those academics of the bourgeoisie whose own interests run counter to those of the working class. Postmodernists are either committed to undermining the theorizing of capitalism, as being a totalizing power, accusing it of being an archaic perspective which constructs a centralizing view of power relations, or they see capitalism as simply being permanent.

Radical theory and popular politics as witnessed in some forms of anticapitalist movements arguably have been affected by postmodernism and its pessimism over the possibilities or desire for a socialist society. The effect is to influence the anticapitalist movements, like, for example the World Social Forum, into being anticapitalist without adopting the view that capitalism needs to be abolished (Gilbert 2008). After all, from a postmodern perspective, power is not concentrated in one place, but is everywhere.

Since the mid-1990s there has been a growing opposition to specific features of global capitalism and its institutions. These groups often oppose the work of the World Trade Organization and the North American Free Trade Agreement and reject the globalization of the economy when its motives are purely for corporate profit. The World Social Forum has been said to be the organization where this opposition appears to converge (Gilbert 2008) and where the most authoritative statements of the values that lie behind these protests reside. In documents like their Charter of Principles (2002) they declares that

- The World Social Forum is a plural, diversified, non-confessional, non-governmental and non-party context that, in a decentralized fashion, interrelates organisations and movements engaged in concrete action at levels from the local to the international to build another world.
- The World Social Forum is opposed to all totalitarian and reductionist views of economy, development and history.
- The alternatives proposed at the World Social Forum stand in opposition to a process of globalisation commanded by the large multinational corporations and by the governments and international institutions at the service of those corporations' interests, with the complicity of national governments.

Here anticapitalism is constructed as being opposed to the hegemony of capitalist practices but the charter denies the need for the single objective of 'smashing' capitalism and replacing it with some pre-formulated society structure. As Gilbert makes clear:

> Although contemporary anti-capitalist groups are often prepared to fight institutions by any means necessary . . . , they are not committed to the arguably impossible goal of over-turning all existing social relations and are not committed to a singular vision of an alternative. (2008:77)

Once again 'a plural, diversified, non-confessional, non-governmental and non-party context' (World Social Forum 2002) borrows a postmodernist pessimistic position on the forms of change that are possible or desirable. It seemingly rejects and finds 'mind-boggling' the very notion of fundamental transformation of society and the destruction of capitalism in the same way as postmodernist and post-structuralist academics perceive the prospects for socialism.

A Marxist response to this would be class-based and unambiguous. Marxism perceives this form of anticapitalism to be utopian and typical of middle class liberal ideals (e.g., Woods 2008). For Marxists, the perception of globalization – which often forms the focus to demonstrations and resistance in the anti-capitalist movement – is a not a new phenomenon and has not been properly understood by those involved in protests against it. Marx and Engels explained that capitalism must always find 'new markets for its products, chasing the bourgeoisie over the entire surface of the globe'. Yet, although capital has achieved this expansion in the most brutal and unjust ways, from a Marxist point of view this achievement is a symptom of an ongoing progressive development of human society, and it lays the foundations for a qualitatively higher stage of human development – world socialism (Woods 2008). Marxism is part of modernism's insistence in a belief in movement, progress and the evolution of societies through history.

Marx, as a left Hegelian, drew on Hegel's use of dialectics to theorize this ongoing movement of change. Dialectics is the methodology Marxism uses for thinking about the world of nature and society. It begins with the axiom that all things are in a state of constant flux. Things often appear to be motionless, but careful analysis of processes both at the micro and macro level disproves this misnomer. Dialectics explains that these changes and the motion found everywhere often act in contradiction and this means that progress cannot advance in a smooth linear progression. Instead, processes of change can be interrupted by explosive moments – both in the natural world as well as within society – disruptions that can divert slow accumulated change into rapid periods of acceleration. However, the central premise of dialectics is that everything – both within the macro and micro processes of all existence and from the molecular to the mighty – is in the process of change, motion and development. Dialectics for Marxists is essentially the most general law of nature, a dynamic interpretation of the processes that occur at all levels of organic and inorganic life. The global expansion of capitalism is part of this flux and the progress and development it brings. It will inevitably lead to the conditions that make possible another epoch-changing shift brought to being through the explosive forces of revolution and the advent of genuine world communism and a classless society.

The anticapitalist movement and its demands would be perceived by Marxists as feeble, sentimental, moralistic and lacking a conscious scientific analysis. It is ignorant or dismissive of the materialist conception of history (see Chapter 1) and is lacking a clear demand for international socialism. Marxists would applaud protest and resistance on the streets towards institutions of capital, but insist on shaping demands through an understanding of how societies have and will advance. From a Marxist point of view, the roots of the anticapitalist movement's demands lie in social democratic liberalism and reformism, which arguably saw their golden age after the Second World War and are themselves redundant.

Radical Literacy in a Postmodern World

As I explained in Chapter 1 in my discussion of Marxist perspectives, much contemporary literacy theory has defined models of literacy as stretching across a continuum between ideological and autonomous (Street and Street 1991).

> Literacy can only be known to us in forms which already have political and ideological significance and it cannot, therefore, be helpfully separated from that significance and treated as though it were an 'autonomous' thing. (Street 1984:9)

Autonomous models see literacy as being a unified set of specific skills that can be taught and applied across all contexts. The ideological model sees literacy as only existing within a social context. Literacy is a social practice and is grounded within social, historical cultural and political contexts. From this perspective, literacy is many things and not one and a perspective which questions any attempts to promote one form of literacy as being universally superior.

This perspective follows Foucault (1980) in that literacy is part of the multiple power relationships at work within a society and among people. Practice that emerges from these perspectives tends to emphasize the importance of encouraging students' and teachers' careful consideration of the ideological assumptions behind the form of literacy that is taught and tested (Larson and Marsh 2005). Instead of privileging the particular literacy practice being taught in one's own culture, all stakeholders need to 'suspend judgement as to what constitutes literacy among the people they are working with until they are able to understand what it means to the people themselves' (Street and Lefstein 2007:42).

Street and others are part of New Literacy Studies (Gee 1996, Street 1993) which consists of a body of scholarly work, with an ethnographic perspective, that challenges traditional reading and writing pedagogy. It uses, among other analytical tools, this autonomous and ideological model of the literacy spectrum. It attempts to 'offer a solid framework for building upon what pupils bring with them from home and community' (Street 2003:37) and provides bridges between the community literacies and those of the school. Home literacy accomplishments are celebrated, enabling platforms for reflection on differences and similarities within these cultural practices, rather than just delivery of one autonomous model (Street 2003).

Fairclough (1992) draws heavily on Foucault's (1984) post-structuralism to argue that there is a power struggle within society to control language. Many of his views resemble some of Street's and the ideas of New Literacy Studies. Language is socially determined, and that language will vary from one social situation to another. Fairclough describes language-use as being discourse – language that has ideological meanings embedded within it (see the discussion of post-structuralism earlier in this chapter). Control of the discourse enables easier domination of society by those who maintain power. Fairclough introduces the concept of 'Critical Language Awareness' (CLA) as a practical approach to the study of language and as 'a resource for developing the consciousness of particularly those people who are dominated in a linguistic way' (1992:9–10). CLA demonstrates the ways in which language practices are invested with power and ideology and criticizes mainstream language study as obscuring the ideological investments made in language by powerful forces (Fairclough 1992). Fairclough advocates CLA as 'a prerequisite for effective citizenship and democratic entitlement' (1992:12).

From a Marxist left perspective, this last political aim would seem rather feeble, too modest and smacks of reformism rather than revolution. Although recognizing power and domination within society, this power is identified as being partially, but importantly, linguistic, rather than economic. The identification of the source of power which controls language is avoided, presumably, following Foucault's outright denial of any totality or centre to power. This perspective is reflected in Fairclough's ultimate aim for this form of language study. Fairclough, unlike Marx, fails to lay the blame upon the base of society as being the source of domination. In effect, Fairclough argues for manipulation of the essential parts of the superstructures as a way to mediate power relations in society.

In literacy practice that emphasizes these postmodernist forms of theoretical approach, the model of power offered by these scholars is one that is opaque and diffuse. Social inequalities are driven by dispersed sources and are manifested in inequities of race, class, gender, ability and sexual orientation (Larson and Marsh 2005). Unlike Marxist analysis, class is only one of multiple divisions in society upon which power is exerted upon by the powerful. Struggle is never totalized into a struggle of the named 'working class' against a named 'ruling class' wherein Marxists would argue all dominated subgroups can be found. Instead, cultural domination has replaced class exploitation, arguably diminishing the centrality of class in its analysis of power. The assumption is made that culture can win independence from economic forces through local community educational and pedagogic actions that prepare cultural links between local literacy practices and those provided by an, arguably, impoverished and culture-orientated curricula.

This form of postmodernist literacy education can be criticized by Marxist left proponents as follows:

- It is never explicit about what these forms of pedagogy can do to transform society – what can it change?
- There is no explicit or implicit declaration of the threat that this pedagogy poses to the present socio-economic system and base of society – arguably, capitalism could still function with literacy pedagogies that celebrate differences in literacies.
- It will often suggest engaging with present curricula without challenging the political and economic motivations behind them.

- It can be both explicit and implicit in its acceptance of the empowerment found in traditional literacy curricula provided other literacies can be included – this has been called the 'literacy myth' (Graff 1979).
- It unapologetically has a social democratic liberal reform agenda – there is no suggestion of the need to remove capitalism to herald a more equitable society – change, if that is its motivation, can be gradual.

Class-Based Critical Literacy

Chris Searle's (1998) literacy teaching in the East End of London is famous for its more class-orientated position and acts as an interesting comparison with contemporary radical literacy teaching models. Searle was initially dismissed from his London school for publishing a book of children's poems, 'Stepney Words', against the instructions of the school governors. Searle was later reinstated, after children from his school went on strike and marched to Trafalgar Square. He was also supported by parents; the Inner London Education Authority; fellow teachers; the National Union of Teachers and other Trade Unionists. Governors at the school had judged the children's poems as being too gloomy and emphasizing the darker side of the children's lives in Stepney.

Searle (1975) celebrates how the children's writing he encouraged demonstrated class-consciousness. Searle describes how he decided to develop

a scheme of work in our English lessons which would encourage and nurse these instincts, and would bring the children towards literacy within a real movement of alliance with the oppressed of their neighbourhood, country and world. (1975:8)

The children's writing (Searle 1975) all display animosity towards a common enemy – the ruling class, capitalism and its effects upon their local community. Searle seems to have directed the children's attention to what Marx called the 'base' of society. Much of the children's writing that came as a result of Searle's pedagogy is less concerned with emphasizing the possibilities of releasing linguistic freedom – challenging Standard English conventions or traditional genres and elevating local community language use. The work shows how the meanings the children conveyed in their writing demonstrated class-consciousness and understanding of how capitalism operates and oppresses the working class. Less emphasis is given to the oppressive nature of language itself and instead insights are offered into how traditional literacy practice can reflect forms of resistance. An example from an 11-year-old demonstrates the class nature of their writing:

Rich Luxuries

Why did Taylor Woodrow build the hotel?
When there are so many people who have nowhere to dwell,
The tower Hotel is only for millionaires
There is nowhere for us to live and play.
In the Tower Hotel they have their waitresses
Where we have to slave for ourselves,
They have luxuries galore
Our homes are just a bore.
They have 836 rooms in the hotel
Where we are scrambled up in about four.

Lynn Marles, 11

Searle (1975) writes about the importance of a single 'angle of vision adopted by the teacher and his pupils in the classroom' (p. 8). He discounts the myth that teachers must be objective observers and instead is open about his class allegiances.

> That was the framework of the ideology adopted in these classes . . . within that view the priority was that these working class children should learn to read, write, spell, punctuate, to develop the word as a weapon and tool in their inevitable struggles for improvement and liberation for them, and the rest of their class all over the world. (Searle 1975:9)

This Freirian perspective (see Chapter 7) adopted by Searle does not attempt to construct power as polymorphous in its source and distribution, including language use as central to this diffuse notion of power. Instead, this perspective emphasizes the centralized nature of power and control into capitalist class relations as was described by Marx. Searle makes the Marxist assumption that the children he taught already were class-conscious and aware of the power divisions within society. His role, it seems, was to galvanize these class perspectives and fraternally encourage further development, rationalization and understanding of the class nature of society. In effect, to create what Marx has called 'revolutionary ferment'.

Searle's practice is in contrast to contemporary literacy practice influenced by postmodernism, which draws on Foucault (1984) and others

(Luke and Freebody 1997, Janks 2000, Comber 2001) to understand the role of language in the diffuse patterns of distribution of power and oppression. Descriptions of practice (Larson and Marsh 2005) demonstrate, like other postmodern methods of educational transgression, a reluctance to name sources of domination and inequality, which Searle does unequivocally. 'Social justice' (Vasquez 2005) is a term often applied to efforts made for a fairer society and the emphasis is on negotiation and recognition of difference rather than consolidation under the umbrella of class. Unlike Searle's methods, the practice implies what Lather (2001) would call a 'praxis of not being so sure' (p. 45) that has 'obligations to openness, passage and nonmastery' (2001:184). For example Vasquez describes her approach to literacy thus:

> Working from a critical perspective, my desire was to construct spaces where social justice issues could be raised. Negotiation and contestation were a central part of the discussions rather than a more familiar pattern of discovering the best way. (cited in Larson and Marsh 2005:50)

Vasquez goes on to describe how an issue arose in her class about the exclusion of vegetarians at the school barbecue. Vasquez describes how discussion had previously arisen about MacDonald's use of rainforest land to graze cattle reared for burgers and the injustice of this towards the animals and people who had previously lived in the forests. A worthy and thought-provoking discussion led to how the wording of the promotional flyers for the school barbecue had excluded vegetarians as it assumed everyone would eat meat.In relation to the discussion about MacDonald's, a greater emphasis is given to the superstructures of society rather than to the base. A source of injustice is never identified. This could be described as a left literacy pedagogy, essentially anticapitalist in its awareness of capitalism's hegemony, but like anticapitalist street politics, with no essential will nor strategy to look for the means to remove capitalism forever. Yet, like much of postmodernist philosophy and politics, it rejects any one truth that can direct how to act in the world that would be for the benefit of all (Atkinson 2002).

In this chapter, I have provided a brief description of postmodernist and post-structuralist positions. I have attempted to link these philosophical ideas with left politics and contemporary movements for change. I then went on to show how the views of postmodernism and post-structuralism have impacted left literacy pedagogy, and I made comparisons with other radical models of literacy pedagogy. The aim of this chapter has been to provide a theoretical foundation for understanding influential literacy practice. In Chapters 7 and 8, I return to the ideas of postmodernism and post-structuralism to understand contemporary models of critical literacy practice. I hope that understanding some of this basic philosophy will help readers interpret and analyse the practice.

Chapter 4

Fashioning a Language of Critique

I intend this chapter to form a bridge between the political, philosophical and ideological first half of the book and the second half, which explores how various literacy practices have been informed by the perspectives that I have discussed. I will offer a language and framework of critique for contemporary literacy practice in order to understand its political and ideological origins and consequent objectives. To do this, in the second half of this chapter, I will present a broad typology of literacy pedagogic approaches that has been informed by Bernstein's (1990) typology of pedagogic styles. Like Bernstein's, the typology I present will be classified by two dimensions, one of which is Bernstein's conception of invisible and visible pedagogy which contributes to my measure of the nature of the literacy pedagogy's political affiliations. The second dimension is based on the pedagogy's objectives and overall will to transform society. I will also attempt to justify these forms of measures as a way to analyse the politics of different literacy practices. The left credentials of literacy pedagogies will then be presented for scrutiny in the remainder of the book by using the typology as a lens through which the literacy practice is passed.

First, I begin with a brief discussion of literacy pedagogy's affiliation with politics. I present this discussion now because, at this point, I believe we should remind ourselves of how literacy and language teaching has been seen as central to offering a lever to efforts to sculpt and/or change society by producing an intellectual change either in human individuals or between them. In the first four chapters of this book, as part of my discussion of different political perspectives, I have touched on the links between them and approaches to literacy and understanding culture. Here, I want to explicitly examine why and how literacy, as a subject of study, has been seen to have so much political significance.

Words and Power

The written word can subdue, deceive, pacify, and lull, or it can arouse, enlighten, stimulate and awaken depending on the ideology and practice employed. In short, education can be for domestication or liberation. (Bee 1980:47)

Do we really know all we are doing when we teach children to read and write? To what extent is it a liberating or a repressive activity? By asking questions like these, we begin to politicize the notion of literacy and invest it with an ideological meaning. As a result literacy teaching every day in schools is also about legitimizing certain forms of social relations in particular contexts that exist historically and within certain configurations of knowledge and power (Giroux 1987).

With the exception of those who conceive language to be an autonomous, innate ability hardwired into our genetic development independently of culture (Pinker 1995), language has been seen to be invested with power in a number of ways. As we saw in Chapter 3, Saussure (1916) makes the claim that words – spoken or transcribed – are signifiers that bear no relation to any reality in a primary world. The meanings they produce are generated ideologically within the cultural context within which they are used. One of the consequences of this process of culturally constructed meaning-making is that our very consciousness is formed from the meanings we produce: 'as we learn to speak we enter the world of consciousness, a world created by others before us . . .' (Beakin 1996:26). This inevitably leads to a question of power and the notion of dominant ideologies investing words with their meanings as a way of controlling populations within cultures and societies. For Marxists, this power and ideology has a central source. In Chapter 1, we saw how Marx contended that the relations of production create the base of society's power: 'the real foundation of which arises the legal and political superstructure' (Marx and Engels 1969). It is from this foundation that definite forms of social consciousness and intellectual life are formed. After Marx's death, Engels (1970) made it clear that although the economic base provided the conditions of intellectual activity, it did not mean that this was predictable or mechanically determined (Holborow 1999). However, Marx and Engels (1974) were certain that:

The class which is the ruling material force of society is at the same time its ruling intellectual force – their rule is not only in terms of social and economic power but also in terms of the disproportionate weight in the production and distribution of ideas. (p. 64)

Thompson (1990:1) describes ideology as 'meaning in the service of power'. The Russian Valentin Voloshinov (1973), a Bolshevik, Marxist linguist, in describing words as signs or signifiers, defined signs as that which 'represents, depicts or stands for something outside itself' (p. 9). He was convinced of the ideological nature of all signs. 'The domination of ideology', Voloshinov said, 'coincides with the domain of signs. They equate with one another. Wherever a sign is present, ideology is present too. Everything ideological possesses semiotic value' (1973:10). As a Marxist, Voloshinov sourced the ideology to the base of society. However, Voloshinov argued against the linguistics of Saussure (1916) (see Chapter 3), which Voloshinov contended effectively converted language into 'an inviolable, incontestable norm which the individual had to accept' (p. 52). He believed Saussure's theory robbed language of any creative dynamism. So although consciousness is 'bathed by' signs which piece together and distil experience (Holborow 1999) and although this may be distorted by ideology, language is learned within a context it can be fashioned by, providing utterances with meanings that have what Voloshinov called a particular 'evaluative accent'. This perspective offers a platform for resistance that, he argues, Saussure effectively closed down. It has also been argued (Holborow 1999) that Voloshinov's perspective avoids the circularity of language determinism that stems from Saussure and is taken up by post-structuralism (Foucault 1979a, Wodak 1996, Fairclough 2002).

As we have seen in the previous chapter, post-structuralists argue that not only does language play a part within society, but is constitutive of it. Language can create reality, and Foucault (1979a) goes as far as to suggest that discursive practices are all encompassing, as discourse creates and reproduces all power relations within society. Foucault's work, as we saw in Chapter 3, has influenced such writers as Fairclough (2002). Fairclough advocates what he calls Critical Language Study (1992) in schools. For him, language practices are imbued with power relations and ideological processes of which people are often unaware. He criticizes language study that takes these conventions at face value and obscures their political and ideological investment (Fairclough 1992:7). Fairclough argues that

- language is socially determined and varies according to the social situations within which it is used.
- Discourse helps to constitute and change knowledge and its objects, social relations, and social identity.
- Discourse is shaped by relations of power and invested with ideologies. (1992:8)

If words, as signs, are invested with ideological meaning by the dominant cultures or classes that govern society then it can be argued that literacy teachers need to recognize that they take sides (Rosen 1982), politically and educationally, when they teach literacy that either neutralizes or discloses language's affinity with ideology. By adopting mainstream methods that ignore or promote pedagogy that treats the discourses in society as neutral, one takes a political position, just as one adopts a political position by attempting to resist these discourses by offering, perhaps, a more critical approach in one's literacy teaching, as Fairclough and others suggest. How literacy and language is taught is on fire with politics, whether one is a conservative, post-structuralist or a Marxist. This means that a seemingly normal day-to-day literacy routine in the classroom is alive with ideology and politics, and this conceptualization of literacy teaching forever changes the meaning of what teachers do.

Functional/Traditional Literacy on the Left and Right

Bee (1980) writes that functional literacy can be summed up as a way to make 'people become more productive and efficient citizens under the prevailing governments' (p. 47). A functional literacy is often based and presented on the notion that literacy is autonomous of cultural or political contexts and therefore ideologically neutral. Functional literacy transmits a set of skills from teacher to child, often beginning with what would be considered 'the basics' and then continuing along a clearly defined and demarcated linear path of lessons led by specific learning objectives. It is often 'intensive rather than extensive, selective rather than widespread, geared to employment rather than culture, and a first step towards producing qualified working power' (Berggren and Berggren 1975).

Skills-focused
Unitary view of literacy likely
Acquisition seen as result of individual learning
Learning seen as transferable
Literacy may be measurable
Literacy relatively fixed
Literacy intrinsically value free

FIGURE 1   Functional Literacy (adapted from Hannon 2000:37)

One could argue that this form of literacy education is often fixed by an ideology of conservatism and an objective of social reproduction as it wishes to contribute to the maintenance of the present social structures of society. It presents language as a neutral set of skills that it is necessary to learn so as to gain further forms of capital both within and outside school. The levels of language skill deemed necessary are often determined by predicted futures of the individual.

> Functional literacy is more a donation to the people, a creation by experts which is handed down to selected groups to serve the definite purpose. The educational contents and methods are adapted to keep the participants at a level which the donors consider desirable. Its originators are often closely allied to private business enterprises which have financial interests in developing countries. (Bee 1980:48)

Yet, it is by-no-means conservative educational thought alone that advocates a more traditionally led literacy education promoting the learning of the disciplines of autonomous literacy skills. Some will argue, for example, that a functional approach which puts an emphasis on skills can be learned alongside other more practice-focused perspectives on literacy. This approach emphasizes that the skills of literacy can only be practiced in a context and that an awareness that literacy still exists in many cultural forms makes a compromise of practice possible. Hannon suggests:

> The desire to understand literacy is sometimes best served by focussing on the many different ways in which written language is used within social groups to achieve a variety of purposes but at other times it makes more sense to focus on the commonalities, particularly in how literacy is acquired. (2000:38)

Hannon needs to explain what he hopes will be achieved by his compromise of literacy practices. The objectives are everything in terms of defining the political dimension and affiliation of the practice. Some forms of literacy pedagogy that appear conservative in practice are radical in their aims.

Antonio Gramsci, the Italian Marxist, saw literacy as being a double-edged sword. It could be used for the purpose of social empowerment or for the reproduction of repression and domination (Giroux 1987). Gramsci believed that the subordinate classes needed to free themselves from their dependence on the bourgeois intellectuals in control of schooling and then to develop and disseminate their own conception of the world and of life (Borg et al. 2002). To do this, Entwistle (1979) relates how Gramsci advocated what can only be described as a pedagogy and curriculum more at home in traditional conservative visions of education. He saw workers' and peasants' language practices as being part of inadequate cultural resources; he wanted the subordinated classes to accumulate and engage with truths that had already been discovered and considered as valuable; he contended that the traditional view of academic standards needed to be maintained and learned and he glorified didactic pedagogy (Borg et al. 2002). Gramsci, like his Russian revolutionary contemporary Lenin, saw knowledge and culture as being autonomous, which if taught to workers and peasants could lead to 'a homogenization of opportunities and outcomes in basic education, and eventual full participation in a cultural milieu of the highest order' (Borg et al. 2002:12).Unlike Lenin, however, Gramsci called for a democratization of classical education in prerevolutionary circumstances (Broccoli 1972) as part of a capitalist education. Gramsci's vision was of a conservative education to serve radical ends. It was Gramsci's dedication and determination in creating a Marxist revolution that led him to demand such discipline and rigour from education. Gramsci wrote:

> ... if our aim is to produce a new stratum of intellectuals, including those capable of the highest degree of specialisation, from the social group which has not traditionally developed an appropriate attitude, then we have unprecedented difficulties to overcome. (1971:43)

One could argue that this approach to literacy education and education in general would lead to what Bernstein (1996) described as 'individual enhancement' (p. 6). Like Gramsci, he advocated that education for all would include 'a condition of experiencing boundaries, be they social, intellectual or personal, not as prisons, or stereotypes, but as tension points condensing the past and opening possible futures' (Bernstein 1996:6). Bernstein was not a Marxist, but his critique of present pedagogy was motivated by what he saw as the unequal distribution of children's rights to participation within the social order of education with its 'boundaries and tension points'. He thought children had the right to see themselves included within that educational order (Bourne 2004).

Gramsci, on the other hand, went much further, seeing the socialist movement's cause as being reliant on the transformative power of ideas. He also conceptualized individual enhancement through education as leading to interindividual effects which would in turn lead to the transformation of society. The function of literacy was to prepare for revolution through an exchange of ideas. Radical change could only come about by the elaboration and dissemination of an alternative world view. I will discuss these Marxist perspectives further in Chapter 8.

The Politics of Literacy

Gramsci and others maintained that the skills of reading and writing have rested in the hands of a ruling elite or class who use this literacy to elicit awe from those who do not possess such skills (Hoyles 1977). Scholes (1985) added useful practical examples of this phenomenon. He wrote that the field of education is divided into two categories of study: literature and nonliterature. The former is valued and the latter is often considered beneath our notice. These categories are traversed and supported by another division – the production and consumption of texts. Consumption, Scholes says, is always privileged over the production of texts in classrooms.

> At some level we accept the myth of the ivory tower and secretly despise our own activities as trivial unless we can link them to a reality outside academic life . . . we cannot produce literature in classes, nor can we teach its production. Instead, we teach something called creative writing – the production of pseudo-literary texts. (1985:5)

Hoyles (1977) quotes Trotsky (1975:18) saying: 'In my eyes authors, journalists, and artists stood for a world which was more attractive than any other, one open only to the elect'.

These perspectives describe a process of 'othering' by the structures, parameters and rules of elite literacy accomplishments when education practice presents literary texts as being sacred and untouchable. As a way of trying to understand how this detachment and alienation from literacy occurs, O'Neil (1977) argued that reading is often taught as if it were another language from another world instead of being the highly abstract form of the language of which children have had tacit knowledge for a good part of their lives. 'Pushing reading into context-less space is the first phase in the destruction of coherence' (1977: 77). This form of teaching, O'Neil says, erases intuitive connections. He suggests that we:

> Make a distinction: being able to read means that you can follow words across a page, getting generally what's superficially there. Being literate means you can bring your knowledge to bear on what passes before you. Let us call the latter proper literacy; the former improper. You don't need to be able to read to be properly literate. (1977:74–75)

Neil Postman writes: 'If you cannot read, you cannot be an obedient citizen. An important function of the teaching of reading is to make students accessible to political and historical myth' (1973:22–23). So, forms of resistance do not always take the shape that Gramsci suggested – working class colonization of powerful ways with words. Other resistance strategies (Willis 1977, Apple 1985) are often advocated. Some challenge the traditional sites, structures and forms of traditional literacy and creative activity. They demand the enhancement and promotion of semiotic forms derived from the environment and consciousness of oppressed classes and cultures and that reflect this agency in, for example, vibrant use of nonstandard forms of language. Indeed, Harold Rosen (1982) was a staunch believer that the working class could produce a culture of their own and there were 'other forces at work' (p. 205) than the ideologies that control schooling and the promotion of a literary canon.

The perspectives that I have described above, provide examples of how literacy is central to a politics of education. Learning a prescribed or autonomous literacy can be utilized to either facilitate the means to power and liberation or as a way to detach sections of society from a conception of language that can produce this power, and move these sections towards a disabling and alienated state of being. As I have tried to show, the source of the politics of literacy lies in the essential affordance of language to make meaning and the struggle of control of these meanings through ideological intervention by those with power or through the resistance offered by language insurgents to challenge this power. According to the arguments above, literacy education can either confirm or resist powerful ideologies, making political distinctions between pedagogy both possible and salient. In making these distinctions, I want to argue, that power, ideology and political motivations can be exposed and either embraced or challenged.

Towards a Typology of Literacy Practice

In this section, I attempt to construct, with the help of Bernstein (1996) and Bourne (2004), a broad typology for literacy teaching which differentiates between forms of pedagogy and the foci of the practice in terms of what its practitioners hope to achieve politically. We have seen that more seemingly traditional or conservative forms of literacy practice can be introduced in order to affect radical and revolutionary change. I hope to show, by using Bernstein's theoretical positions, that seemingly progressive literacy pedagogy can have more conservative social outcomes and conversely, some traditional pedagogies can be utilized to produce radical outcomes, thus blurring the distinctions between left and right in literacy education. This perspective will contribute to the construction of a typology which may assist in categorizing literacy practices in ways to differentiate its political affiliations.

Theory of Pedagogic Practice

Earlier in this chapter, I described how Bernstein saw individual enhancement obtained through education as being:

A condition of experiencing boundaries, be they social, intellectual or personal, not as prisons, or stereotypes, but as tension points condensing the past and opening possible futures. Enhancement entails a discipline. (1996:6)

I compared this view with that of Gramsci's – that of being prepared to engage in traditional curriculum and pedagogic forms in order to control and manipulate new knowledge for more radical ends. Bernstein did not anticipate or demand Marxist revolution in the way Gramsci did, but he did believe in individual enhancement, inclusion and participation – education as a collective undertaking – as a way to bringing some form of social transformation (Bernstein 1996, Bourne 2004). Personal change could occur, Bernstein contended, by an education that facilitated the appropriation and remaking of knowledge.

One of Bernstein's concerns was the way knowledge was constructed. He distinguished between, what he called, horizontal and vertical forms of discourse. Horizontal forms of knowledge and discourse are described by Bernstein as: 'the form of knowledge usually typified as everyday, oral or common sense knowledge'. It is 'local, segmental, context dependent, tacit, multi-layered, often contradictory across contexts but not within contexts' (1996:170–171). Vertical discourse, in contrast, 'takes the form of a coherent, explicit, systematically principled structure, hierarchically organized, or it takes the form of a series of specialized languages (Bernstein 1996:170–171). Schools respond to external pressures, by selecting and regulating the knowledge they wish the children to imbibe (Bourne 2004). Schools are oriented towards specific outcomes. By their attempts to establish classified competences or performances they take their significance from the future and not the present (Bernstein 1996). Vertical discourse is embedded within pedagogic discourse of schools and horizontal discourse forms part of informal and local contexts. The former Bernstein describes as having a strong classification – it is strongly framed – very clearly aimed at specific social ends. There is little opportunity for 'local classroom negotiation, either for teachers or pupils' (Bourne 2004:63). Bernstein also shows how this strong framing can be either made explicit to all involved, or hidden. The more explicit forms of approach are often associated with the more transmission-based forms of pedagogy. Progressive forms of education, Bernstein argues, sometimes associated with social democratic liberal ideas (see Chapter 2) often mask the framing of the schooling project. The explicit forms allow understanding of the goals and social aims and the implicit masks the reasons for what is practiced. As Bourne (2004) shows, the more explicitly framed pedagogies are not always conservative in their overall aims. This concurs with my discussion, earlier in the chapter, of Gramsci's work which will be discussed in more detail in Chapter 7.

To put Bernstein's position in leftist Marxist terms: both progressive and transmission forms of pedagogy are integral to the superstructures of society. Progressive forms of teaching may hope to change education processes that encourage more social democratic liberal ends to their work. Yet, neither progressive nor transmission models are concerned with changing the base of society, which for Marxism, is the source of the divisions of power and inequality within society. For Bernstein both forms of pedagogy created the conditions for further social reproduction because of their integral social class assumptions. I now need to explain this a little more.

Social Class Assumptions of Pedagogy

In pursuit of an understanding of the imbalance of achievement between social classes in schools, Bernstein attempted to explore what he saw as social class assumptions that permeate the pedagogies employed in classrooms. Sociologists like Bourdieu, Apple and Bernstein have tended to agree that schools are organized and run by the middle class and that the practices found therein are saturated by its cultural discourses and assumptions. However, within the middle class itself, principles and values are not always agreed upon. Bernstein (2003) describes how factions of the middle class are often at loggerheads over principles of social control. This manifests itself in arguments over the role of the state in society and consequently influences relations in schools. It is worth quoting Bernstein at length here:

> On the whole the middle class sponsors of invisible pedagogy (which will be discussed later in this chapter) support state intervention and the expansion of agents and agencies of symbolic control, and thus the growth in public expenditure. For this is the ground and opportunity of their own reproduction and advancement, whereas the middle-class sponsors of visible pedagogy drawn from the economic sector and the entrepreneurial professions are opposed to growth in public expenditure. Thus, there are opposing material and symbolic (discursive) interests. (2003:212)

According to Bernstein, forms of pedagogic relations in classrooms are manifestations of the values of two different factions of the middle class. The forms of cultural relay that are supported by these factions of a culture are seen as ways to assist in the social reproduction of their own cultural selves.

> He (Bernstein) differentiates between the pedagogic practice that is dependent on the economic market – that emphasises vocational education – and another that is independent and autonomous of the market – that is legitimated by the autonomy of knowledge. (Sadovnik 2001:11)

In the chapters preceding this one, I have attempted to conceptualize these middle class approaches politically as neoliberal and social democratic liberalism respectively. Bernstein (2003) attempted to show that whatever the practice promoted by these two factions of the middle class, present class inequalities are likely to be reproduced as both factions promote the interests of the middle class or dominant class. Indeed, both factions of the middle class have no interest, unlike Gramsci, in utilizing pedagogy as a weapon to attack the base of society – capitalism. This leads inevitably, as Bernstein contends, to the social reproduction of the inequalities of capitalist society.

Pedagogical Rules

Bernstein proposed that the 'essential logic of any pedagogical relation consists of the relationship essentially between three rules' (2003:64) – hierarchical, sequencing and criterial (see Figure 1). The hierarchical rules refer to the relationship between the transmitter and the acquirer, a relationship governed by rules of social order, character and manner that condition the conduct in the pedagogic relation. The sequential rules are the ordering and the pace by which the transmission is expected to be made. The criterial rules enable the acquirer to understand 'what counts as legitimate or illegitimate communications, social relations, or position' (Bernstein 2003:65) in the pedagogic relations. Bernstein calls the hierarchical rules the regulative rules and the sequential and criterial, instructional or discursive rules. When the criterial rules are strong it also means that the teachers have less control over the 'how' and 'what' of school activity themselves.

Bernstein contended that there are two generic types of pedagogic practice. If the regulative and discursive rules are explicit he calls this type of pedagogy *visible* (VP). When the rules are implicit the pedagogy is *invisible*(IP). In Figure 2 the three rules are categorized into implicit and explicit forms and consequently into invisible and visible pedagogies.

Rules of pedagogic practice	Explicit (Visible Pedagogy)	Implicit (Invisible Pedagogy)
Hierarchical (Regulative)	Power is clear subordination and superordination	Power is masked Teacher acts directly on contexts and indirectly on acquirer
Sequencing (Discursive)	Regulation of development is clear. Child always aware of expectations and his/her own progress	Teacher only is aware of child's development and expectations of progress
Criterial (Discursive)	Objectives and criteria for success is made clear to child	Child is unaware of objectives and criteria for success other than they are implicit, multiple and diffuse. Children can operate with minimal external constraints

FIGURE 2 The Three Rules of Pedagogy

Underachievement – Invisible and Visible Pedagogy

Bernstein's analysis of the social class assumptions of teaching practice link the micro-educational processes to the macro-sociological aspects of the social structure of society (Sadovnik 2001). 'Bernstein contributed to a greater understanding of how schools reproduce what they are ideologically committed to eradicating – social-class advantages in schooling and society' (Sadovnik 2001:17). As the wars between different factions of the middle class continue over pedagogy and power, other social groups – namely the working class – arguably continue to lose out. For Marxists, Bernstein provides an analytical framework which illuminates the weaknesses in manipulating and attempting to transform the superstructures of society – in the form of education and pedagogy – without attempting to affect the base. Using Bernstein's perspectives, working this way will have minimal effects on inequality of achievement and its consequent reproductive impact on social class and mobility. Bernstein implicitly provides a warning for the working class to look beyond schooling within capitalism for liberation. His analysis of the affects of both visible and invisible pedagogy on the working class was revelatory in many respects.

Visible Disadvantage

For Bernstein, disadvantages for working class children derive from issues of time and space. Using visible pedagogy, sequencing rules are explicit and clearly mark the future of the child's development in demarcated steps. The pace of this sequence is often consistently brisk. Bernstein contended that for the academic curriculum to be acquired there need to be two sites of acquisition – school and home. This supplementation to the school day in the form of homework requires an appropriate space and a commitment and understanding of the pedagogy applied. Some families, often from poorer homes, do not have the economic capital to provide these resources and therefore 'failure becomes an expectation and the reality' (Bernstein 2003: 72).

The tendency for failure in school is also seriously exacerbated by a lack of orientation to the linguistic styles common with the school's pedagogic community. 'The pacing rule of transmission acts selectively on those who acquire the school's pedagogic code, and this is a social class principle of selection' (Bernstein 2003:73). This disadvantage, in terms of, what Gee (2001) calls the primary discourses also means that children from homes where the discourse does not match those of school will require more time and greater determination to 'tune in' to the powerful discourses associated with academic success. The pace of the pedagogy is so great that there is a tendency for these children to lag behind others.

Invisible Disadvantage

With the use of invisible pedagogic relations, inequalities also persist. Bernstein argues that the surface features of visible pedagogy can be understood by all. It is a standard pedagogic form, often replicated in many family homes. Bernstein has always been clear that pedagogy occurs in many sites and is not unique to school and other official educational institutions. The home is also a key site of pedagogical relations. Bernstein describes pedagogy thus:

> Pedagogy is a sustained process whereby somebody(s) acquires new forms or develops existing forms of conduct, knowledge, practice and criteria, from somebody(s) or something deemed to be an appropriate provider or evaluator. (1996:78)

For example, in each room of the family house operating with a visible pedagogy, a particular function is bestowed. Within these rooms, objects may have fixed positions and spaces may be reserved for people or things. In homes with a more invisible pedagogy operating, space is more weakly marked. The rules that regulate the movement of things are less constraining. Living may be more of an open plan. Like the home operating a visible pedagogy, Bernstein argues, cognitive and social messages are carried by the spaces. Invisible pedagogies both in school and at home require more space and they presuppose more movement by those concerned. 'When the spatial requirement is translated into family space it is clear that the family cannot employ an invisible pedagogy where there are members confined to a small space, as is the case with many working class and lower-working class families' (Bernstein 2003:75). In addition, families that operate visible pedagogies at home punctuate time by a series of dislocations and expected behaviours. Invisible pedagogies offer a very different temporal grid which may appear alien to children from homes where time is treated very differently and is more explicitly controlled.

Invisible pedagogy that is competence-oriented and intraindividual (top left-hand quadrant) is described by Bernstein as being a 'masked pedagogy'. Although these pedagogic formulations appear to provide weak selection, pacing and sequencing rules, and while children are given more choice and autonomy, developmental learning theories also require teachers to covertly evaluate children's productions against selected fixed norms of attainment. The responsibility for success or failure is given to the child in evidence of their natural capacities (Bourne 2004). In this environment, in effect, evaluation replaces instruction and deprives children of key aspects of cultural capital, which those children from dominated classes are unlikely to find at home. Here again, the middle class are given an advantage.

Change – Intraindividual	
1. Social Democratic i) Progressive/Romantic: Theories based on shared competencies (masked pedagogy). ii) Post-structuralist positions on literacy. Critical Literacy Studies (masked/blurred political ends). Not a framed political focus.	2. Conservative – Neoliberal: Behaviourist learning theories. Functional skills–based practice. Autonomy of culture and literacy.
3. Radical: Revolutionary Critical Literacy Neo-Marxists – Freire Giroux Slow 'revolutionary ferment' 'Wars of position'	4. Marxist Revolutionary Gramsci's position on literacy and culture. Literacy and educational practice not the most important priority for change. Gramsci and Lenin on culture and explicit framed focus. Literacy – autonomy of both. Russian Bolsheviks before 1924. Hatcher (2009)
Change – Intergroup	

(Left axis: Invisible Pedagogy; Right axis: Visible Pedagogy)

FIGURE 3 Typology of Literacy Pedagogy. Adapted from Bernstein 1990 and Bourne 2004

In Figure 3, I draw on Bernstein's typology to move towards one for literacy practice which will help guide us through the second half of this book. This second half aims to analyse a range of literacy pedagogy, and in so doing, I also follow Bourne's work (2004) in her use of Bernstein's typology for developing a 'radical visible pedagogy'. However, I wish to critique the version of radical pedagogy that Bourne offers and replace it with a Marxist 'take' on radical visible practice. My typology in Figure 3 replicates Bernstein's vertical axis, representing the type of change the pedagogy aims to achieve (intergroup to intraindividual). However, in contrast to Bernstein's and Bourne's, the 'intergroup' change that both of my bottom quadrants wish to instigate is a Marxist revolutionary one. The horizontal axis represents the literacy pedagogy's adherence to the explicit (visible) or implicit (invisible) rules of its practice. In further recognition of the typology's presentation of specifically literacy pedagogy, three of the quadrants contain more than one form of approach to literacy practice, but which, I believe, conform to many of the same rules of pedagogy and therefore can be categorized in a similar fashion.

In the top left-hand quadrant 1 can be found the social democratic (see Chapter 6 for further discussion) invisible pedagogic practices. Broadly speaking, the teacher is given the task of being more of a facilitator rather than transmitter of knowledge and the children are generally encouraged to progress at their own pace. As I have explained, Bernstein argues the pedagogy is masked. The children are required, as part of the developmental learning theories from which these practices derive, to be regularly evaluated. Evaluation here replaces instruction and children are not given access to both the results of these evaluations or, more important, to the vertical discourses on which much the evaluations are informed.

The second group in this quadrant also wish to valorize disadvantaged groups' knowledge as part of an invisible pedagogy, relaxing the pacing, sequencing and evaluation rules. Yet, unlike quadrants 2, 3 and 4 there is a blurred, unspecified political objective – there is no framed focus to their educational practices which, as I argued in Chapter 3 is often typical of postmodernist and post-structuralist positions. They do wish to change the general hierarchical nature of literacy teaching, exposing the ideological nature of conceptions of literacy and curriculum, but they make no explicit reference to the object of this dissent, that is, the base of society capitalism. Arguably, like other aspects of invisible pedagogy, this is another form of masking, either consciously or unconsciously, of a more implicit conservative project that mirrors the political and reproductive motivations of other forms of invisible, 'progressive' pedagogy. Attitudes to sources of power and domination being dissipated and plural, as the postmodern position contends, leads to a paralysis of action and objective, which arguably creates political stasis.

All the literacy pedagogic positions represented in quadrant 1 arguably tinker with education as part of the superstructure and do not attempt to challenge the base of society.

Quadrant 3 shows a form of neo-Marxist acquisition-orientated pedagogy that Bernstein represents in his typology. 'In which the content pacing, sequencing and evaluation rules are relaxed and in which the voices, knowledge and understanding of politically disadvantaged groups are valorized' (Bourne 2004:65). Yet, this form of invisible pedagogy also has an explicitly framed revolutionary objective: the Marxist revolutionary transformation of society. As Bourne (2004) points out, however, Bernstein's theoretical lens provides a unique perspective on a possible error in these pedagogue's project as Bernstein would argue that 'local valorisation of disadvantaged groups' knowledge in this evaluative context can only lead back to masked pedagogy' (Bourne 2004:65). As with the masked pedagogy offered in quadrant 1, and using the same criticism that Gramsci made (which I covered earlier), stratification of teaching leads to acquirers being offered 'operations, local skills rather than the exploration of principles and general skills and the pacing is likely to be weakened' (Bernstein 1990:77).

Quadrants 2 and 4 share the explicit nature of the project of their pedagogy. Both are open about their political and social ends, although both are diametrically opposed ideologically. In quadrant 2, a functional, skills-based literacy practice is advocated, where achievement is individualized and openly competitive and where success and failure are associated with social class background (Bourne 2004). However, as Bernstein would contend, in both quadrants 1 and 2, inequalities arise when forms of 'cultural capital' are missing for individual children from the working class, or, as Bernstein argues, a lack of a second space for pedagogy, namely, the home.

In quadrant 4, a Marxist revolutionary objective is central to the philosophy, while in quadrant 2 the reproduction of existing social structures under a capitalist society dictate the pedagogy. Both forms of pedagogy in quadrants 2 and 4 conceptualize literacy and culture as autonomous. The pedagogy would see the acquisition and control of the powerful forms of educational discourse as crucial to the transformation of society through the destruction of capitalism and the introduction of democratic socialism. All the pedagogic rules are explicit, offering a visible pedagogy. Crucially, however, this Marxist quadrant contains two attitudes to literacy and education in capitalist societies.

(i) Contemporary and historical approaches to Marxism (e.g., Trotsky 1980, Hatcher 2007), which propose the relevance and salience of the 'materialist conception of history'. Such approaches lay less emphasis on the affordances that education can provide in terms of creating the conditions for the transformation of society. Adaptation of the superstructures of capitalist society has little real or lasting impact on the conditions of the working class. For these Marxists, a rich and meaningful literacy education could only occur in a post-revolutionary situation (see discussion in Chapter 8).

(ii) However, Marxists like Gramsci, as I explained earlier in this chapter, take the second perspective. He did advocate a visible pedagogy in prerevolutionary capitalist conditions as he saw this as being crucial to contributing to the 'war of position' for which Lenin had little time (Fitzpatrick 2002). Although teachers like Freire (1996) (represented in quadrant 1) followed the Gramscian position on education within capitalism, Freire advocated a pedagogy that can be categorized as invisible. As I will show in Chapter 8, his approach was centred on the democratisation of education practices. It is because Gramsci perceived literacy and culture as autonomous that his perspectives must sit in quadrant 4.

So, in a very real sense, the first Marxist approach to literacy and education in quadrant 4 could conceivably exist outside of the four quadrants. As I have already mentioned in Chapter 3, a literacy that takes a left position in terms of its objectives has no real meaning in a capitalist society for this Marxist position. Events on the local and world stage will have a far greater effect on the consciousness of the working class than any form of schooling – should a radical form be given the space to function. The materialist conception of history contends that as conditions worsen under capitalism the consequences will be events of such a cataclysmic nature that they will lead the working class to understand their historical destiny which will be to transform society.

Sociologists call this the 'automaticity theory' and have tried to rebuke this perspective with what they call 'relative autonomy theory' (Apple 1985). It could be argued that relative autonomy theory would be comparable to those perspectives in quadrant 3. This theory holds that teachers can manipulate and subvert the time and space in traditional schooling to offer a pedagogy that can resist the dominant ideology of capitalist education (more on this in Chapter 7). However, for Marxists, the inevitability of world events shaking the working class into the development of a revolutionary class consciousness means that radical schooling and education are both unlikely and unnecessary. Unlikely, because of the approach taken by the pedagogues in quadrants 1, 2 and 3, and unnecessary in the face of the final epoch-changing events associated with the fall of capitalism. Of course, Marxists like Luxembourg (1970) have always applauded the efforts made, within the limitations of the capitalist system, by social reformers and those in the field of education who seek to ease the burden and subjugation of the working class. Yet, at the same time, Luxembourg was determined to make it clear that reforms in capitalism are reliant on the buoyancy of the economy and will inevitably be temporary or superficial.

Finally, I wish to discuss Bourne's (2004) call for a radical visible pedagogy which she forms from Bernstein's (1990) conceptualization of the
bottom-right quadrant (4), which in my own typology I have called 'Marxist
Revolutionary'. Like in my and Bernstein's typologies, Bourne explains
that the difference between the conservative forms of visible pedagogy and
the visible pedagogy in this quadrant is its objective, which is to encourage
the 'collective access to and participation in academically valued social
practices and the discourses by which they are constituted' (2004:66).
Learning in Bourne and Bernstein's quadrant 4, foregrounds the collective
nature of learning rather than the individual attainment found in quadrant 2,
whose objectives are competitive, producing differences between learners
and creating hierarchical rankings. However, for Bourne and Bernstein,
one must always be wary of positioning children within 'segmented horizontal discourses' (Bourne 2004:73), as the pedagogies in quadrants 1 and
3 encourage. Here, learners are unlikely to be able to have access to the
analytical power provided by what has been an elite educational discourse.
It is for these reasons that Bourne advocates what she calls a radical visible
pedagogy. Yet, I would argue that Bourne's vision of pedagogy appears to be
advocated within the existing base of capitalist economies and therefore is
susceptible to the objectives and manipulations of its superstructures.
In addition, the distinction that is made between Bourne's position and
the position of radical pedagogues in quadrant 3 is her insistence on an
emphasis on vertical discourse as part of the explicit nature of the pedagogy. However, she does concede the need for more 'openness' (p. 66)
between teachers and students and the 'managed' introduction of horizontal discourses in order for students to culturally connect with their
teachers. Here, she is in danger of falling into progressive, social democratic liberal approaches and therefore her arguments become susceptible
to criticisms from both traditionalists and progressives. The progressive and
post-structuralist objection to her position can be demonstrated by Bourne's
example of a teacher utilizing a radical visible pedagogy: her determination
to insist on standard uses of English by her students. Children in her class
describe incidents of this occurring:

> She will stop us and say 'No, look, what do you mean by that? Don't talk
> like that, say that again.'

And

> I don't think she minds us talking how we talk because that is us, but she
> wants us to know when to stop. (p. 72)

Fairclough (1992) would argue that this is what he calls 'an appropriateness model of language'. Teaching that one form of language is better, or more appropriate in more prestigious and powerful contexts like schools and universities and other formal arenas, eventually makes some children's habitual community language use seem marginal and irrelevant. In addition, children from environments that already use this kind of powerful discourse will be immediately advantaged and will not have their cultural language identity challenged and labelled as a deficit. Socio-economic class and cultural identities provided for individuals from a capitalist base make this form of pedagogy likely to continue patterns of social reproduction as Bernstein, himself, describes. From a Marxist left position, Bourne's vision of radical pedagogy would only successfully operate after the demise of capitalism. I believe she is correct to place her radical form of pedagogy in this quadrant, but unlike in my version, she does not articulate the necessity of the abolition of capitalism and therefore from a left Marxist position, her vision is flawed.

In this chapter, I have first attempted briefly to demonstrate the political nature of literacy (see Lankshear and Lawler 1987 for a more extensive discussion) in an explicit way. I then offered a typology for literacy pedagogy which is able to identify and classify literacy teaching in terms of its political affiliations and objectives. There is great complexity to the political perspectives of literacy teaching. The typology is an attempt to categorize types of literacy pedagogy in a way that begins to unravel some of this complexity. I shall be drawing on the typology in Figure 2 in the remainder of the book to analyse the political nature of a number of forms of pedagogy and determine their left or right credentials. I hope that by doing so, I will allow readers to begin to grasp the range of perspectives for the teaching of literacy on the left.

Part II

Politics and Literacy Practice

Chapter 5

Conservative Discourse and Literacy Practice

We have come to the point at which we can begin to use the theoretical frameworks from the first half of the book to make a political analysis of examples of literacy practice and the policy from which it derives. This chapter will examine practices that I want to argue fall into quadrant 2 in my typology found in Chapter 4. (In the later chapters, I will be describing forms of practice that lie in the other quadrants to help establish a clearer understanding of literacy teaching from a political dimension.) These quadrant 2 practices have the objective of intraindividual development in functional skills-based learning. They use visible pedagogic approaches and are typical of neoliberal market-driven literacy teaching. In this chapter, we will be studying literacy that is certainly not on the left of the political spectrum. I will start this process with what is described as a 'typical phonics lesson' (Macnair et al. 2006) and I will explain why I believe this form of literacy practice is an element of a conservative discourse in education under capitalism. I hope to demonstrate, by drawing on insights from Chapter 2, how what appears to be a common form of literacy lesson found in many schools in England and elsewhere, is in fact alive with political significance and is an integral element of the contemporary neoliberal project within Western developed capitalist states. By offering this kind of analysis, I want to add an extra politically vibrant dimension to our gaze on this form of pedagogy. In the second half of the chapter, I will discuss this modern approach to literacy, and the policies and policy documents from whence it comes, to try to understand contemporary schooled literacy and its classed objectives.

Synthetic Phonics

I have chosen to examine one teacher's approach to the teaching of synthetic phonics. This approach is taken from an edited book (Lewis and

Ellis 2006) which aims to support teachers and student teachers in their understanding of phonics methods in primary schools (Macnair et al. 2006). The book is recommended (Harrison 2006) for its impartial approach to describing contemporary practice in phonics teaching and for 'offering opinions based on reliable and proven evidence' (Bearne 2006:160). The lesson which is described here cannot be said to be completely 'typical' of most phonics lessons, but contains a pedagogy that advocates of phonics would perceive as being an example of 'typical' good practice. It is this form of pedagogy that I wish to analyse, recognizing that there are alternative versions of phonics teaching of which Lewes and Ellis also provide examples and which I have critiqued elsewhere (Lambirth 2007).

The forms of teaching children to read and to spell using phonics have been associated with traditional methods of teaching literacy (Coles 2000). Drawing its ideas on practice from cognitive–psychological educational theory (Ehri 1987, 1995), it is based upon the belief that children need to be introduced to specific skills and knowledge in literacy at specific ages, as it is assumed that all children should be taught to progress in similar ways. It conceptualizes literacy as 'autonomous' (Street 1984) (see 'Introduction' and Chapter 3) and pre- scribes the teaching of basic skills 'especially those that take apart sounds within words, connect sounds to make words, associate sounds and letters and identify sight words' (Coles 2000:x). In England, in response to criticism of the teaching of reading, particularly during the late 1990s and early twenty-first century, the British government commissioned what they called the 'Indepen- dent Review of the Teaching of Early Reading' (Rose 2006) – known as the 'Rose Review' – which recommended the teaching of phonics for children from the age of five or even younger. Rose wrote that:

> Beginners should be taught grapheme-phoneme correspondence from simple to complex and in a clearly defined incremental sequence. . . . Children's mastery of the decoding and encoding skills taught up to any given point (grapheme-phoneme correspondences, blending and segmenting) should be frequently assessed and appropriate teaching should be provided for those who need it. (2006:2)

Using synthetic phonics, the individual phonemes associated with particular graphemes are each isolated, pronounced and blended together (synthesized) to read and write a word. For example, p/a/t has three phonemes and three graphemes, and the word b/r/u/sh is made from four phonemes. Children are taught to *segment* words into their individual phonemes. Segmentation is seen by proponents of synthetic phonics as a way to assist children to spell. The belief is that children need to segment a word they want to spell into its component phonemes, providing a grapheme (letter) or combination of graphemes to represent each phoneme (its sound). Teaching synthetic phonics also entails instructing the children how to *blend* a word. This means merging the phonemes together to pronounce a word. When confronted with an unknown word while reading the children are taught to attribute a phoneme to each letter or letter combination and then merge them to sound out the word.

The method of teaching reading by synthetic phonics has been challenged by educationalists (Wyse and Styles 2007, Goouch and Lambirth 2007, Wyse and Goswami 2008, Goswami 2007) for what they see is a misreading of the research in the field by the proponents of synthetic phonics and by the conclusions and forms of practice that are constructed from its use. I will not be concentrating on this form of analysis and critique; instead, I wish to examine the practice using a political analysis.

The teacher in this example (Macnair et al. 2006) describes her induction to the teaching of synthetic phonics. She had observed in-service training sessions in Clackmannanshire, in Scotland, where research (Johnstone and Watson, 2003, 2005) into the teaching of early reading using this method has been undertaken and has been very influential in the findings of the Rose review (Rose 2006) and in the implementation of policy. Macnair describes how she had been very impressed by the pace of the lessons and by the children's enthusiasm to engage in this form of pedagogy. 'Having observed the lessons and read the teachers' materials I was keen to begin. I started with a small class and developed a blue print which I now use with most classes I teach' (p. 46). Macnair stresses that the children were active in their role in the lessons, having access to the whiteboard, chalkboard or wedge. She describes the children's seating positions as 'sitting in front of the chalkboard in rows or in a circle with a magnetic board' (p. 46).

Before I offer Macnair's example of her phonics lesson, it is important to mention that the description of her session gives no indication of the age of the children, other than the information that Macnair is an infant teacher. In England, this puts the children's possible ages anywhere between five and seven. Significantly, for this analysis, we are also told nothing about the socio-economic, gender or ethnic background of the children. It would seem from this that readers are to conceptualize the children in the lesson as a homogenous group of infants. Factors of difference like this appear to have little significance for Macnair et al. in their description of the phonics teaching. The model offered here depicts the children as socio-economically neutral, all operating on a culturally and economically equal basis.

This would be typical of cognitive–psychological educational theory (Ehri 1987, 1995) which advocates, in most cases, that all children will require the same teaching whoever they are. One may be also tempted to connect this approach with liberal and neoliberal perspectives on society in general that conceptualize people as having an identical and static nature. Social class, race or gender within a classic liberal society (see Chapter 2) has little significance for the way education should be provided by state schools, as it has little bearing on subjectivity or needs. Children are required to learn the cultural currency of the day in a nonnegotiated, efficient and identical manner – a metaphorical inoculation of a form of 'positive knowledge' (Cusick 1983, Giroux 1997).

Macnair's typical lesson lasts from between 30 to 40 minutes. It consists of six components:

- Warm-up
- Revision
- A new sound
- Word making
- Letter formation
- Consolidation

The warm-up involves the children singing a number of songs and playing games that name letters and reinforce some of the previous learning. The revision section is a form of interactive test of the degree to which the children have retained knowledge from the previous session, and it prepares them for new information. Macnair reports: 'At this point I remind them that to read a word they need to sound and blend it' (p. 47). This is, of course, far from being an indisputable truth; it is an extremely contested position and for many would be seen as misleading. Yet, this method of teaching is born from a positivist epistemology, and for its efficiency to be realized there is no time to negotiate or debate the reliability of the knowledge it relays. Integral to the mechanism of the teaching is a strong framing of the hierarchical and criterial rules (Bernstein 1996) which are embedded in its action. As we have seen (Chapter 4), this form of pedagogy, which has been called 'visible' (Bernstein 1996), has what Bernstein believes are social class assumptions.

The 'new sound' section involves the teacher taking a letter from the alphabet with 'the explanation that the letter makes a particular sound' (p. 47). This too has been contested by some (Strauss and Altwerger 2007) who argue that in addition to letters (often vowels) having a number of variants on the sound they represent, the English phonics system acts at a level of complexity that defies teachability. So, in truth, the teacher's statement is again questionable. However, the children in this section of Macnair's lesson are given a physical action to perform that represents the sound the letter makes and words are shown to the children that contain the grapheme with the phoneme. Quickly, the children are asked to utilize this new knowledge: 'I then ask for examples of words containing the new sound and write them on the board' (p. 47). The emphasis appears to be on precision, efficiency and accuracy in the children's responses to the task. The 'word making' and 'letter formation' sections introduce more reinforcement and another form of testing of the children's individual application of the knowledge that they have been given.

In 'consolidation', children are given a number of challenges and problem-solving activities that involve the use of individual letters to make words. Macnair reports the children take great pleasure in the activities and gain great satisfaction using their newly acquired knowledge. All the activities with letters appear to be in isolation from full texts within which they may be found in, arguably, more meaningful contexts. Indeed, these discrete ways of teaching phonics were part of the recommendations of the Rose Review (Rose 2006).

In attempting to politically understand this form of literacy teaching, it is important to contextualize this lesson in terms of its political and economic place in history. One must accept that it happened in the beginning of the twenty-first century, in a state school in Britain which has a capitalist economy hungry for more flexible, functionally literate workers to fill places in a changing work force. From a Marxist perspective, capitalism must ensure that those available to work have particular forms of labour power (see Chapter 1) for employers to buy as a commodity from the individual. This enables business to draw off the crucial 'surplus value' that makes profits.

As we saw in 'Introduction', literacy taught in the way Macnair advocates fits well into the model prescribed by New Labour educational policy for literacy. Instead of literacy being a way to access other forms of learning, mastering literacy itself instead becomes the central objective for primary school children (Lankshear and Knobel 2003). Changes in the forms of skills needed in new forms of industry in the twenty-first century demand that individuals must have effective labour power for these new kinds of employment. The need for greater levels of functional literacy makes the efficiency of the pedagogy employed to reach these new standards extremely important.

As I have said, Macnair's pedagogy would sit in the top right-hand quadrant (see Chapter 4) of my typology for literacy teaching. Achievement within this model is generally individualized. Although the children have some opportunities to work in pairs in the final section of the lesson, they are provided with a transmission-based form of pedagogy that they receive individually as they sit in rows or in a circle around some form of writing board. Time is provided for individual children to demonstrate their levels of understanding by undertaking a number of short testing exercises. Responsibility for authority is securely and explicitly in the hands of the teacher. Indeed, all the rules of pedagogic practice (Bernstein 1996) are visible and explicit – hierarchical, criterial and sequential. There is also an extremely brisk pace to the lesson, typical of a visible pedagogy as described by Bernstein (1996).

The pedagogy described here has all the qualities that Bernstein (1996) would associate with a perspective drawn from those who value and have dependence on the economic market. Its main objective is to equip children with functional forms of literacy by transmission of specific skills that the teacher represents as ideologically neutral and unquestionable. It is a functional literacy that is presented as 'a donation to the people, a creation by experts which is handed down to selected groups to serve the definite purpose' (Bee 1980;48). Macnair's pedagogic model has few of the qualities of invisible literacy pedagogy found in quadrants 1 and 3 of my typology for literacy teaching. For example, the objectives are clearly not interindividual, as they are in quadrant 3. There is no expectation or will for children to be learning about reading and writing which creates bonds between individuals, groups, cultures or classes through contexts or the texts they study. The overwhelming drive is for individuals to be equipped with discrete and decontextualized skills. From Bernstein's (1996) perspective, Macnair's teaching contains all the social class assumptions which, according to Bernstein, form part of all visible pedagogy and, consequently, creates serious social and political consequences for working class students (see Chapter 4).

The Neo-Marxist educator Freire (1996) described teaching such as that offered by Macnair as having what he called a narrative character. School classrooms contain a narrating subject (teacher) and listening objects (students). The teachers describe reality as 'if it were motionless, static, compartmentalized and predictable' (p. 52). This is similar to the analysis of transmission forms of pedagogy that O'Neil (1977) draws on. Pedagogy like the one Macnair describes, – for, Freire, is decontextualized for the children. In Macnair's case, her method appears to introduce aspects of the children's everyday language in ways that represent it as unknown, alien and unusual. With the exception of what children can represent from the previous lesson, the children's knowledge of language, as constructed by this session's content, is conceptualized as being in deficit. In taking this approach, O'Neil would argue, much of the coherence and the intuitive connections children try to make with new knowledge is undermined. For Freire, this kind of teaching turns children

> into 'containers', into 'receptacles' to be filled by the teacher. The more completely she fills the receptacles, the better a teacher she is. The more meekly the receptacles permit themselves to be filled, the better students they are . . . education becomes an act of depositing . . . this is the banking concept of education. (1996:53)

Freire argues that this concept of education projects an absolute ignorance onto the learners, which he describes as being characteristic of oppression and oppressive and hegemonic regimes. It removes the notion of education and knowledge as a process of enquiry and constructs politically useful oppressive power relations between authority and subjects. Freire believed strongly in the reconciliation of teacher and student as being able to both share the role of teacher and learner (Freire 1996). This places Freire and his followers into the radical quadrant of my typology for literacy. He too will be critiqued in some detail in the following chapters.

Politically, Macnair's phonics lesson is embedded deeply into conservative social reproductive forms of cultural relay whose pedagogic rules (Bernstein 1996) place her methods into a contemporary neoliberal project with clear economic and social objectives under capitalism. This is not to condemn the teacher as a conservative or neoliberal herself, but her pedagogy, whether she knows so or not, can be categorized in this way and arguably contains many elements of clear political objectives.

Conservative Neoliberal Phonics

As we have already seen from Chapter 2, neoliberalism as a form of capitalist policy and control offers an explicit approach to establishing the relationship between the state, the market and different sections of society. Drawn from the classical liberalism of the early eighteenth century, it highlights the supremacy of the individual, the market, rationality, efficiency and the individual acquisition of skills.

Classic liberalism had a profound belief in 'self-ownership' and that individuals were responsible for their own well-being and advancement.

The state's role under a neoliberal regime is to ensure the individual citizen's right to follow their innate drive to succeed, and to offer the opportunity to gain the skills needed to prosper in society in the most efficient and regularized manner. Using this political logic, a contemporary cultural currency needs to be dispensed through schooling to equip prospective workers to be able to feed the market with the skills and labour power required for a healthy industrial work force.

Macnair was looking for an efficient 'blue-print' for her teaching of reading and she realized it in her six-section lesson. It is channelled towards efficiency and is marked by speed and the testing of the individual children's accuracy. Her model provides no space for negotiation with the children, as the content provided is supported by a self-assured businesslike rationale. Her epistemological approach to her methods of teaching and the contents of which she relays is positivist. It is positivist in the way there is a separation of values from knowledge – an implied objectivity. This appears to be the secret of Macnair's perception of the efficacy of her methods. There is simply no place in terms of time or space for contemplation of alternative approaches that are inclusive of other values and judgements made from other cultural, political or social perspectives; the 'facts' that drive the pedagogy and the content that it carries are looked upon as objective and value-free. Giroux (1996) contends:

> Guided by the search for reliability, consistency, and quantitative predictions, positivist educational practice excludes the role of values, feelings, and subjectively defined meanings in its paradigm. Normative criteria are dismissed either as forms of bias or are seen as subjective data that contribute little to the goals of schooling. (p. 19)

According to Shannon, what he calls 'the efficiency movement' in reading instruction began during the first two decades of the twentieth century (Shannon, 1989). He quotes from the early 1900s: 'Primarily schooling is a problem of economy; it seeks to determine in what manner the working unit may be made to return the largest dividend upon the material investment of time, energy, and money' (Bagley 1911:2). Shannon (2001) is an educationalist working in the United States. He describes how, like in the United Kingdom, a rationalization process in education in the United States has brought high-stakes tests which demand that teachers avoid the punishments handed out to schools that do not reach the expected scores, by introducing reading programmes and teaching scripts that provide a greater opportunity of success in the tests.

The 'rationalization' of reading instruction is only part of the spread of capitalist logic throughout public and private life. According to this logic in order to reduce the risk to capital and to maximize profits, all aspects of business must become predictable. This is not as easy as it might seem because people, raw materials, the environment and capital are involved in production. (Shannon 2001:2)

Dudley-Marling and Murphy (2001) state that business in the United States has transformed different literacies into commodities for students to acquire in order to increase their market value later when seeking employment. This business logic encourages hierarchical relationships of authority, an analysis of the means needed to reach specific ends, and continuous regulation to ensure predictability in institutions. Shannon believes that 'rationalization, then, treats human beings as variables to be manipulated along with materials, time, and space to ensure predictable products and profits from material, ideational or social manufacturing' (2001:3).

Macnair's teaching, as we will see, exists in a similar political context and under the same pressures from high-stakes testing. Her 'blue-print' for phonics teaching operates in much the same way as the programmes and scripts that Shannon describe as being central to this form of approach to schooling. It attempts, using this business logic, to provide a clear predictable result from her instruction. It ignores many of the significant differences and the similarities that humans may possess that may interrupt the flow and continuity of her work in an effort to create the most efficient and reliable model.

Efficiency is one essential feature within a neoliberal ideological framework. As we have seen (Chapter 2), neoliberalism conceives the state as a means to providing the conditions, laws and institutions for the effective organization of society. In this vision, the state is used to make individuals enterprising, competitive and proficient. Education and schooling must be perceived by those who use it, to be a sound investment in terms of the skills and training it offers. It must appear to offer optimum means for future success. Consequently, from this perspective, all rational people will opt for schooling and the forms of 'positive knowledge' that are offered there to help guarantee individual success in the market.

Advocates of the neoliberal-inspired Human Capital Theory (HCT) (Fitzsimmons and Peters 1994) wish to encourage a 'training culture' that emphasizes skills as the basis of value in a competitive market. The approach to reading presented by Macnair et al. (2006) and other forms of functional literacy offers a regularized training model for the efficient transmission and capture of skills. The children in the example I described, passively receive these skills unquestionably, implicitly trusting the forms of positive knowledge they gain. Yet as discussed in Chapter 1: 'capitalism needs workers who are clever enough to be profitable, but not wise enough to know what's really going on' (Wrigley 2006:2). It might be argued that training provides this kind of worker at the expense of the encouragement of more critical and questioning members of society. The description of the children's passivity corresponds to Marx's definition of labour power as the aggregate of mental and physical capabilities (see Chapter 1). Labour power represents the capacity of a person to work in a particular society, but it also describes mental capabilities. One could argue that the children in the example are not only being trained in the discrete skills to distinguish phonemes represented by graphemes – thus being made ready to effectively become readers – but they also have acquired particular attitudes and dispositions. These may include a passive reliance on an unquestionable hierarchy. There is also implicit encouragement to consider one's own individual success as a learner to be crucial, while, as a result, essential connections and solidarity with others are discouraged.

Neoliberal/Capitalist Literacy Policy

Since the early 1990s in Britain and the United States, policies for the teaching of reading and writing have been characterized by an emphasis on 'what works' for individual children in schools. These policies, I want to argue, help to explain the efforts of Macnair in her class room and others in the United States and the United Kingdom to establish prescribed methods that have the greatest impact on the largest number of individual children. In 1996, the incoming New Labour education secretary in the United Kingdom declared that teachers were to 'use teaching methods which work and are not the latest fashion' (Rafferty 1996). In a statement in 1997, the New Labour party declared that they would 'encourage the use of the most effective teaching methods, including phonics for reading' (Labour Party 1997:8). Thus, the Literacy Task Force was set up in 1996 to explore how a more 'back-to-basics' method of teaching reading could be established: '. . . teachers must be crystal clear as to what their pupils need to know, understand and be able to do to become confident and proficient readers' (Ofsted 1996a:93). Many of the policy and inspection documents began to dispense with references to pleasure and to the joys of reading and concentrated on efficiency, skills and accuracy. The policy settlement that occurred as a result of numerous reports of underachievement in England and Wales (Education, Science and Arts Committee [EASC] 1991, Turner, 1990, Alexander et al., 1992, Ofsted 1996a) culminated in the National Literacy Strategy (NLS) (DfEE 1998). This document provided teachers with a framework for how to teach reading and writing. It provided a set of learning objectives for each year group in primary schools and a clearly defined model of teaching literacy within what was called a 'literacy hour'. Since then, phonics in the early years of literacy teaching has taken an even more significant role in the teaching of literacy in primary schools than the National Literacy Strategy originally suggested. The Rose Review (2006), as mentioned earlier in this chapter, advised that schools should adopt teaching programmes that introduced synthetic phonics in ways similar to Macnair's lessons and that these should be 'followed faithfully' (Rose, 2006:18) – in other words, one must suppose, 'uncritically'.

As we saw from Shannon's work, in the United States a similar approach to reading pedagogy and an insistence on the use of the teaching of phonics as the most efficient way of teaching children to read has also been popular with governments and policy makers. Between 1985 and 2000, the United States government ordered three separate reports (Snow et al. 1998, National Reading Panel 2000) on reading to assist the formation of policy. All came out broadly in favour of phonics as the prime method for teaching early reading. The Bush administration accepted the report 'as justification for the Reading First Initiative within the No Child Left Behind iteration of the Elementary and Secondary Education Act in 2002' (Shannon 2007:68). It would appear that there was and is a continuity and duplication of policy for literacy teaching in both the United States and parts of the United Kingdom, and this same policy can also be found in Australia (DEST 2005). Such policy drives the practice I have described in this chapter, and an analysis of this pedagogy should include a consideration of the sources of this approach.

Lankshear and Knobel (2009) offer a postmodern analysis of contemporary literacy education policy with efficiency measured by standardized testing and linked to accountability at the head of its drive to change the outputs and objectives of schooling. Lankshear and Knobel (2009) draw on Lyotard (1993) who explored the perspective that knowledge is always imbued with some form of status and that this status has changed in postindustrial society. According to Lyotard, the change in the status of knowledge has occurred as a consequence of a modification and a loss of belief in the grand narratives of modernity. Lyotard conceptualizes knowledge as a commodity produced in order to be sold and consumed. Knowledge, for

Lyotard, is no longer some thing valued for what it offers in terms of universal truths about, for example, the human condition. Instead, it becomes of use only in what it offers in terms of its exchange value. What knowledge provides in terms of exchange now gives it its value and provides legitimacy for its transmission. Therefore, the relationship between teacher, as a deliverer or supplier, and the student, as a user, is thus transformed into one of a commodity exchange contract. Neoliberal policy makes education one of the state's institutionalized activities. It is there to transmit 'positive knowledge' or acquired learning to those who need it and a school's legitimacy as a centre for this operation is based on the principle of performativity.

> This is the principle of optimising the overall performance of social institutions (like schools) according to the criterion of efficiency. . . . Specific institutions are legitimated by their contribution to maximising performance of the state or corporate systems of which they are a part. In this way, enhanced demonstrable, measurable performance becomes its own end. (Lankshear and Knobel 2009:62)

For Lankshear and Knobel, education has lost its place as part of universal welfare rights based on a social democratic model and has instead been transformed into a subsector of the economy – a business no less. They call this 'being part of a postmodern condition', one to which, I would argue Macnair's (2006) model of phonics teaching and others like it, would also be seen to be a part.

Marxists on the left would want to explain the change of education policy and practice in literacy differently. They would contest the belief extolled by Lyotard that changes in education policy come from some form of subjective change of opinion concerning the 'metanarratives of modernity' or any kind of caprice on the part of those who have power in society. Instead, Marxists will always seek objective reasons based upon an analysis of events in the preceding period (Woods 2008). Marxists would describe neoliberalism as just another form of capitalism. Neoliberalism sits to the right of more social democratic forms of liberalism. This manifestation is not new, in fact, as we have seen in previous chapters it draws on classical liberalism and its current resurrection is simply an expression of an economic system in crisis.

In Chapter 2, I described the Marxist belief that in the period after the Second World War capitalism was once again threatened by the spectre of communism. To counter this danger it offered the working class social democratic welfare reforms and employed Keynesian economic measures which heralded a period of great prosperity. This wealth was mainly brought to being less through Keynesianism and more through an expansion in world trade. From a Marxist perspective, this period of great prosperity from 1948 until around 1974 strengthened the working class. There was a massive expansion in education for all, allowing for more opportunity and greater access to a variety of new and innovative practices. Full employment meant stronger trade unions and a stronger labour movement. However, this period of boom was inevitably followed by a period during the 1970s of high inflation brought on by the application of deficit financing. This caused high deficits and high levels of inflation. Monetarism and the economics of Milton Friedman were introduced to remove the poison of inflation, which wreaked havoc on a capitalist system of economics. The use of the economics of Friedman and what is now called 'neoliberalism' were attempts to return to the old ideas and methods of capitalism in its infancy – pure market economics as they were in the days of the nineteenth century, before governments began to intervene in the workings of the market (Woods 2008).

The literacy pedagogy of the type described in this chapter belongs to this period where the needs of the market are served efficiently, incontestably and religiously. The labour power required to serve this market must be formed as cheaply and as efficiently as possible. With the health of the market as education's main aim, schools must streamline their teaching to meet these pressing demands. The expensive social democratic indulgences of the past, manifested in progressive forms of educational practice have no place in this new economic climate formed to fight the vagaries of the internal contradictions of capitalism. Indeed, some argue (McMurtry 2002) that the present political climate actively ensures the suppression of oppositional critical thought to the measures being applied. Hatcher describes how the neoliberal project in education is being manipulated in an organized and systematic way.

> The business agenda for schools is increasingly transnational, generated, and disseminated through key organisations of the International Economic Cooperation and Development (OECD). In that global context there is a project for education at the European level, which represents the specific agenda of the dominant European economic and political interest. (Hatcher and Hirtt 1999)

The conservative literacy practices I have described in this chapter appear to suit the economic climate of the day.

This chapter has offered a political analysis of a form of pedagogy that attempts to create intraindividual change through a functional skills-based practice, manifesting all the traits of a visible pedagogy associated with market-based economic and political perspectives (Bernstein 1996, Bourne 2004). I want to describe the practice as 'conservative' and typical of a literacy pedagogy operating in contemporary society's classrooms within a system of capitalism. It sits squarely in my own typology, derived from Bernstein's (1996), in quadrant 2. I want to call it broadly right wing within the context of capitalism as, for example, it attempts to create a labour power that can be bought as a commodity to feed an ailing capitalism and help bolster profits and bring down the horrors of inflation. Of course, the synthetic phonics lesson that I provide is just an example of functional skills-based practice. There are others I could have introduced that also represent this model of literacy. Yet, my example does exemplify teaching that offers an autonomous model of literacy and constructs literacy learning as a collection of discrete skills that individuals must acquire. I also want to concede that it offers only a snapshot of one teacher's model of literacy teaching, providing a small indication of the form of relationship that the teacher has with her children. I recognize that there is so much more to observe and understand about any individual's teaching than just one regular teaching routine. In providing an analysis of this teaching, I have drawn on an understanding of political and economic theory that drives education policy and have offered a critique from left-wing perspectives – namely Marxist and postmodernist. In the following chapter, social democratic 'progressive' forms of pedagogy will be examined.

Chapter 6

Social Democratic Liberal Discourse and Literacy Practice

This chapter will examine the forms of literacy practice that sit in quadrant 1 of my typology. It will explore those practices that include social democratic liberal and postmodernist perspectives; theories based on shared competencies and with what has been called masked pedagogy (Bernstein 1996) and post-structuralist positions on literacy without a framed political objective. I will begin by reminding readers of the historical contexts and the mission of social democratic policy and practice. In doing so, I will describe how these forms of practices in a literacy curriculum have been described as invisible pedagogy (Bernstein 1996) and how these ideas are manifested in practice. I shall do this by providing an example of professional development in literacy teaching which attempted to change the practice of the teaching of writing in a number of primary schools in the southeast of England. I will then turn to the work of Mercer (2000) and Mercer and Littleton (2007) on encouraging 'ground rules for talk' as an example of practice operating on the centre right of social democratic educational discourse.

In critical literacy advocate Hilary Janks' book *Literacy and Power* (2010), her final chapter discusses the future of critical literacy in the world that may lie ahead. In the opening paragraph she states:

> In a peaceful world without the threat of global warming or conflict or war, where everyone has access to education, health care, food and a dignified life, there would still be a need for critical literacy. In a world that is rich with difference, there is still likely to be intolerance and fear of the other. Because difference is structured in dominance, unequal access to resources based on gender, race, ethnicity, nationality and class will continue to produce privilege and resentment. (p. 203)

I discuss the concept of 'critical literacy education' later on in this book. Broadly speaking, critical literacy education involves encouraging students to question some of the assumptions behind learning to be literate and to analyse power and domination behind the uses of literacy in society. As I intend to show later, critical literacy can take a number of forms.

In Janks' vision of the future, she appears resigned to the continuation of some of the inequalities that Marxists believe form the basis of a capitalist economy, yet is optimistic that this reformed capitalism can bring peace, wealth and security for the foreseeable future. As a strong supporter of critical literacy, her left political objectives for the teaching she advocates would seem restricted by her lack of revolutionary optimism and zeal. This would be in marked contrast to fellow critical literacy proponent Freire (1996), who made revolution central to his pedagogy. Instead, her picture of life ahead could be categorized as one grounded in a form of 'capitalist realism' (Fisher 2009). From this pessimistic theoretical foundation, there is a resignation that capitalism is here to stay; indeed, from this perspective, it is easier to imagine the end of the world than to imagine the end of capitalism (Fisher 2009). One is resigned to the demise of any hope for the transformation of society based on socialist or communist ideals. Therefore, a critical approach to learning about literacy, as advocated by this form of critical literacy, becomes an essential tool to cope with capitalism's vagaries and to work for its reform, but not, so it would seem, its replacement, which is now unthinkable for many. It is here a distinction can be made between this form of critical literacy and revolutionary critical literacy. The former is very much a part of social democratic liberal reformist traditions and has a conservative element embedded in its resignation about the continuation of the capitalist economy. The latter still aspires to revolution and so the two forms of critical literacy sit in different quadrants of my typology of literacy pedagogy.

Fisher (2009) describes how an 'attitude of ironic distance proper to postmodern capitalism' (p. 5) is used to protect many from the seductions of the ideologies of the past. For Fisher, there is now 'a pervasive sense of exhaustion, of cultural and political sterility' (p. 7) among once more radical sections of society. He argues that in the United Kingdom, since the 1980s and the miner's strike, all hope of a socialist alternative has gone within these groups. Now capitalism is all that is left. Fisher quotes Badiou (2001) and his contention that modern capitalism is presented as 'as good as it gets':

To justify their conservatism, the partisans of the established order cannot really call it (Capitalism) ideal or wonderful. So instead, they have decided to say that all the rest is horrible. Sure, they say, we may not live in a condition of perfect Goodness. But we're lucky that we don't live in a condition of Evil. Our democracy is not perfect. But it's better than the bloody dictatorships. Capitalism is unjust. But it's not criminal like Stalinism. We let millions of Africans die of AIDS, but we don't make racist nationalist declarations like Milosevic. We kill Iraqis with our airplanes, but we don't cut their throats with machetes like they do in Rwanda, etc. (2001:5)

Capitalist realism, as described by Fisher (2009) helps explain how some forms of critical literacy are perceived by many contemporary education academics as one way to steel ourselves to the inevitability of capitalism and may bring 'social justice' rather than revolution. Reform of the education system to provide children with the tools for further reform would, for Marxists, make social democratic liberal critical literacy fundamentally conservative. Although Marxists are not opposed to reform (Luxembourg 1970) they would contend, through recourse to the materialist conception of history and to dialectics, that capitalism's future is far from assured. It can be argued that Fukuyama's (1992) announcement of the end of history is manifested in 'capitalist realism' and lies at the heart of much social democratic educational discourse. The form of critical literacy that Janks (2010) advocates belongs in my first quadrant of social democratic liberal literacy practice, but is just one of a number of manifestations of reformist left perspectives.

Social Democratic Discourses

The literacy practice I intend to analyse in this chapter takes several forms. Most, in comparison with the practice described in Chapter 5, can be perceived as deriving from the political left, in that, all wish to make educational interventions that might enrich and change the lives of the children and empower them individually. Many of the advocates of this form of pedagogy are opposed to much of the policy that comes from contemporary neoliberal governments. Importantly, for their left credentials, most are less explicitly concerned with the demands of the market economy, highlighting personal intellectual growth as the priority over technical skills for operating successfully at work. However, like Janks, there is little hope or desire to rid the world of capitalism. Some have a more aesthetic project – emphasizing the deep pleasures of reading and writing texts. This form of literacy practice has been described as a 'romantic' approach (Freire and Macedo

1987). While others have a more libertarian perspective, empowering through the promotion and celebration of home cultures; advocating the privileging of local literacies and language-use and the building of metaphorical bridges between different forms of cultural capital. Others, I wish to argue, use the rhetoric of social democratic liberal education, but offer a more prescriptive and autonomous view of literacy.

Reformism and Social Democratic Left Literacy Traditions

In Chapter 2, I introduced the rationale and ideas of social democratic liberalism. I described how, during the 1860s, it was deemed crucial that the state intervene in matters of health, welfare and education as it became clear that the unfettered development of markets could not provide adequately for the needs of the growing working class. Often these reforms had come about through sustained pressure from the labour movement, Christian groups, charities and reformist societies. Yet, as some Marxists have pointed out (Brookes 2007), the arbiters of capitalism recognized that improving the general living conditions of workers was in the long-term interests of capitalism because they acted as a metaphorical 'safety valve' preventing serious industrial unrest and action, and providing short-term relief to those living in abject poverty and desperation.

In Britain, in 1884, the Fabian Society was formed. This group is an important example of social democratic thinking and the consequent action that began in the nineteenth century and whose influence can still be found in the modern Labour Party in the United Kingdom today. Since 1997 there have been around 200 Fabian MPs in the House of Commons. At one time, nearly the entire cabinet were Fabians, including Tony Blair, Gordon Brown, Robin Cook, Jack Straw, David Blunkett and Clare Short. The Fabians have been characterized by a commitment to what is typically called 'social justice' and a belief in the progressive improvement of society. At the core of the Fabians was the work of Sidney and Beatrice Webb who published a number of influential works on industrialization and social justice issues in the early twentieth century. They advocated change through reform, not revolution. The Fabians were supporters of the nationalization of land and the introduction of a minimum wage. Yet, to those on the Marxist left, they presented a danger to the revolution and the working class as their ultimate aim was the maintenance of a reformed capitalism.

The Russian revolutionary, Leon Trotsky (1974), although having more time for Sidney and Beatrice Webb than other leading Fabians like Ramsay MacDonald, reminds his readers that 'at the Labour Party Conference in 1923 Sidney Webb recalled that the founder of British socialism was not Karl Marx but Robert Owen, who preached not the class struggle but the time-hallowed doctrine of the brotherhood of all mankind' (p. 54). Indeed the Fabians have always maintained a diversity of opinion, motivated by the desire to stimulate debate rather than to promote a particular political 'line'. Its members would often advocate a union of all classes, underplaying the class-nature of socialism. In a famous quotation, Trotsky, who many still see as having been the one of the most consistent and closest followers in thought and deed of left Marxism says:

> Throughout the whole of history of the British Labour movement there has been pressure by the bourgeoisie upon the proletariat through the agency of radicals, intellectuals, drawing-room and church socialists and Owenites who reject the class struggle and advocate the principle of social solidarity, preach collaboration with the bourgeoisie, bridle, enfeeble and politically debase the proletariat. (1974:48)

The Fabians' commitment to gradual change through the mechanisms of the trade unions and the Labour Party, for Marxists, made them a reactionary force; not because they desired the betterment of the conditions of the working class, but because their control of the Labour movement led to its impotence by destabilizing the class objectives of a working-class party. A belief in the possibility of long-term social improvements through reform under capitalism, alongside an insistence on the need to unite with other classes, would always mean the Fabians and other social democratic liberal organizations work against the revolution and, ultimately, the working class. Trotsky again:

> It can be without exaggeration be said that the Fabian Society, which was founded in 1884 with the object of 'arousing the social conscience', is nowadays the most reactionary grouping in Great Britain. Neither the Conservative Club, nor Oxford University, nor the English Bishops and other priestly institutions can stand comparison with the Fabians. For all these are institutions of the enemy classes and the revolutionary movement of the proletariat will inevitably burst the dam they form. (1974:57)

I have argued in this book that social democratic liberal principles reside within many of the literacy pedagogies advocated by the left. Many have a radical facade and claim solidarity with the working class and other oppressed groups. Yet, like in more general manifestations of politics as described above, there is distinction to be made between a social democratic left which can be conceptualized as fundamentally conservative – working for capitalism's longevity – and the revolutionary left which wishes the demise of capitalism.

Crossing Quadrants

Much social democratic literacy practice has been linked to progressive methods of teaching (Lambirth 2007) which Bernstein (1996) categorizes as being a form of invisible pedagogy. As I discussed in Chapter 4, Bernstein describes how schools are the domain of the middle sections of society, yet, within this middle class, values and principles are not always agreed upon. As I have shown, Bernstein contends that disagreements over principles of social control manifest themselves in the pedagogies that each faction of the middle class advocates in classrooms. Middle class sponsors of invisible pedagogy tend to support state intervention and the growth of public expenditure, while those factions that support more visible pedagogies are often drawn from the economic sector and are opposed to growth in public expenditure. Despite some of the complexities of the reality of classroom principles, the two positions he describes can be compared to the historical and political divisions between social democratic liberal policy and practice and the classic liberal and neoliberal positions described earlier in this book and in the last chapter. For Bernstein (1996), both visible and invisible pedagogy carry social class assumptions which negatively affect the educational development trajectories of many working-class children.

In the typology for literacy teaching that I introduced in Chapter 4, which is based on Bernstein's general typology of pedagogies, social democratic liberal literacy pedagogy is intra-individual in objectives. The teacher is a background 'facilitator', rather than an instructor and children are said to be progressing at their own pace. The regulative and discursive rules are implicit (see Chapter 4). However, although the teacher is not concerned with the gradable performance of the children in the classroom, there is still a focus on the 'procedures internal to the acquirer (cognitive, linguistic, affective, motivational) as a consequence of which a text is created and experienced' (Bernstein 2003:69). Children are provided with more choice and freedom to move within the classroom area. They are in more apparent control of their learning but teachers are still required to evaluate children's work against fixed norms of attainment. 'These biologize children's attainments, and place responsibility for what is perceived as "success or failure" firmly with the child, as evidence of their own natural capacity' (Bourne 2004:64). Bernstein maintains that this masked pedagogy replaces instruction with evaluation in schools and produces learners at individually different levels of competence. The working-class child misses the instruction, which Bernstein argues, is provided for children that are more middle class through access provided by parents who have the means to valued forms of knowledge (see Chapter 4).

As I argued in Chapter 4, Bernstein's work provides further scholarship that contributes to the importance of being aware of the cultural and class contexts within which pedagogy is active. Within a Marxist left analytical framework, the social structures of capitalism (the base) create the conditions (the superstructures) within which power is activated in favour of a ruling class. Some forms of the social democratic liberal literacy pedagogy that Bernstein categorizes so powerfully are often resistant only to the visible pedagogies of their fellow social class travellers. It is politically left in the way that its political foundation lies in the overall social democratic drive to make reforms based around an increase in state expenditure typical of social democratic liberal reformers. This can be illustrated by an example of professional development that I undertook a few years ago. The project's participants, perceived using my Bernstein-influenced typology, were working to cross the quadrants from visible to invisible pedagogy. In other words, one faction of the middle class, supporting particular pedagogies, were attempting to undermine another faction of the middle class's pedagogy. However, the political motivations and drives behind the pedagogy stopped there. The current policy was only to resist more conservative visible pedagogy.

The projects which I wish to describe were undertaken sequentially from 1999. Each hoped to improve the provision for the teaching of writing across the schools. Each had a duration of roughly two academic years. All the schools were in the primary sector and included some junior and infants-only schools. There were 23 schools in total. Using data taken from the schools' last Ofsted reports, 78 per cent of the schools contained children that came from average and above socio-economic home circumstances.

Each development project broadly consisted of the same structure and worked across three stages. Stage one involved an audit which attempted to gauge current contexts in terms of the attitudes and practice of the teachers and children. We provided teacher questionnaires; a children's writing survey, which consisted of questionnaires and interviews for all the children from foundation to year six. These questionnaires were undertaken by the children themselves or given in the form of interviews by teachers or classroom assistants, depending upon the age and experience of the children. Samples of children's work with the teachers' commentaries and some factual information about the school were also taken. Stage two consisted of the development phase which involved the formation of the project focus groups (PFG). Each group comprised two teachers from each school who 'explored their own understanding of creativity in writing, developed their own creativity personally and professionally and worked on various school selected foci' (Grainger et al. 2005). On each project, the tutors also encouraged the teachers to write for themselves. Stage three evaluated the impact of the project and involved a repeat of the initial audit and a celebration conference when teachers from the schools met to share the work with which they had been involved. A final report was written by the tutor team for the head teachers and others involved in commissioning and constructing the projects. Here I shall discuss the second project, which was called 'The Write Voice'.

The title puns on one of the project's broad objectives which were to develop the 'voice' of the child. Various authors (Graves 1983, Bearne 2002, Grainger et al. 2005) have advocated encouraging 'voice' in children's writing. The 'voice' in this context is associated with the imprint of the author's individuality, reflecting 'the ring of conviction of the writer' (Bearne 2002:10) and the culture from which he/she comes. From a Bernstein theoretical perspective, the emphasis of the project was based on the conviction that the child's 'voice' must be heard. The project seeks a more 'horizontal discourse' and positions the teacher as a facilitator for the child's individual expression. The teacher exerts minimal external constraints; the criterial rules are weak as the project seeks the child's self-expression seemingly free from explicit markers to success. Competition is minimized as a result of the view that individuality and difference is an indication of personal creativity. However, in addition, the project is about encouraging 'the voice' in writing. Writing as the medium of self-expression belongs firmly within more traditional school communicative modes and continues to form the medium of assessment and the means to academic success in schools. The project emphasizes writing in preference to, for example, digital literacies and new technological forms of communication that facilitate the use of sound and image. There is a strong symbolic control over the communicative modes based firmly on traditional curricula. Already, the movement of the pedagogy is guided towards a more invisible form, yet set firmly in more traditional communicative modes that arguably favour those for whom these modes are more culturally familiar.

The initial audit, combined with discussions from staff meetings and with the PFG, highlighted issues that the project leaders and the participants wished to address:

- The predominance of the teachers' pseudo and prescriptive learning objective focused questions. (1)
- The need to use content responsive comment/ questions. (2)
- The importance of children's questions. (3)
- The role of the child's own perspective on their writing. (4)
- The value of close analysis of teacher/child talk. (5)

In negotiation with all the participants the foci of the projects were developed. They consisted of the following:

- More collaborative classroom environments. (1)
- More choice and space in writing. (2)
- More positive attitudes to writing. (3)
- Teachers more willing to take risks. (4)
- Teachers developing stronger convictions and deeper understanding of literacy learning. (5)
- Schools more aware of the role of talk in writing. (6)

In both sets of development issues the hierarchical rules are encouraged to be weaker – collaboration, choice, space are where the teacher should be prepared to take more 'risk'. Risk here is associated with a relaxing of rules for the subordination of the children, but also with teachers choosing a more improvisational style of teaching. In issue one of the first participants' targets, the project aimed to remove teacher questioning of the children based on non-context led issues and that emphasized objective external criteria. Instead, these questions were seen as needing to be replaced by those that are based far more on context and issues concerned with individual response. In addition, a weak criterial rule was advocated by encouraging children's own questions and the need to elicit the child's own perspective on their writing. All this contributed to a seeming weakening of sequencing and criterial rules as the children appeared to become more involved in assessment of their own work and the work of others. The issues raised formed part of the project's overall aim which was to create more positive attitudes to the writing by, as Bernstein would describe, weakening the regulative and discursive rules.

The schools developed their own sets of actions plans. Each school's focus could be conceptualized as being at least directed towards a pedagogy with weaker regulative and discursive rules, suggesting a more invisible pedagogy.

- 'response partners and writing journals'
- 'responding to writing and drama'
- 'oral storytelling into writing'
- 'increasing talk to aid writing'
- 'drama and writing were the common foci'

These methods reduced the strength of hierarchical rules through children's own storytelling and dramatic work which would also reduce the extent of external restraints on what they could do. It also reduced the pace of sequencing and enabled the children to use more space in the classroom. However, the projects central focus which was writing – a traditional form of symbolic practice – was always highlighted as the main aim of all these more invisible pedagogic styles.

The final audit revealed that teachers used drama, storytelling and small group talk to encourage writing. In addition, many reported feeling freer and more flexible in being able to think for themselves and choose outside the NLS (National Literacy Strategy) framework. A group of others also referred to their own development as writers. The power relations are reported to have radically changed. The teachers themselves had described feeling less constrained and this had led to what amounted to a weakening of the regulative and discursive rules in their own practice. The audit also suggested more satisfaction as a result of the weakening of these pedagogic rules on the behalf of the children and in the way teachers responded to the children's work. In conclusion to the final report, the authors wrote:

> There is still some way to go to embed the activities into a principled understanding of literacy learning, but it is clear the 'Write Voice' schools have travelled a considerable distance and now demonstrate increased autonomy and creative flexibility in their development and delivery of the schools' writing curriculum. (p. 26)

The teachers and project leaders appear to have made progress in crossing the quadrants of my typology away from more conservative-influenced visible pedagogies and into more progressive, invisible literacy pedagogies. The resistance to a visible pedagogy we offered through the practice we advocated was arguably embedded within social class assumptions that resided in what Bernstein calls the middle class – the class traditionally associated with control of schooling. Our work could be conceptualized as forming part of the factional skirmishes that are a consistent feature within the liberal education establishment. From my own experience, the aims of the project I have described are not untypical of many university-designed professional development projects and, writing as someone who codesigned the project, the social democratic liberal principles of our work were the main driver behind our motivations for making a difference to the schools within which we worked. There was a politics to what we hoped to achieve. There was also a morality based upon our own values and the values of those with whom we worked.

Interestingly, from a historical, political perspective, education in post-revolutionary Marxist Russia borrowed educational theory from progressive thinkers like Dewey (Fitzpatrick 2002) whose teaching approaches would sit in quadrant 1 of my typology. The Soviets strived to introduce curricula and pedagogy that were close to Bernstein's (1996) definitions of invisible pedagogy today. The work we advocated in our contemporary professional development project would have been supported by the commissars of left Marxism. Yet, our context was capitalism and under these conditions, Lenin and his fellow Bolsheviks would have not had the same attitude to the work we undertook.

Dabbling within the Superstructures

The move across the quadrants that the writing project attempted to do with the literacy pedagogy in the primary schools sits in social democratic liberal traditions of reforming capitalism. Those on the Marxist left would argue that it only dabbles with a pedagogy that forms part of the superstructure, which in turn has been formed by the base of society (capitalism) and now works to maintain that base. The left credentials of this form of pedagogy reaches the pinnacle of its radicalism in being a form of reformism as it ignores a number of crucial political and socio-cultural elements that would remain the same despite its work. I have already indicated how, using Bernstein's insights, it ignores the social class assumptions and cultural consequences of the pedagogy it employed. It also functions with further assumptions.

Central to the pedagogy in the example I have shown are classic forms of social democratic liberal thought. As I have indicated, the place of choice for the children, a greater say in the direction of the teaching and an acknowledgement of the importance of individual voice exists alongside, and is embedded within, the traditional literacy practices and the forms of assessment that remained constant. One of the main features of a Keynesian social democracy was the compromise and accord it sought between the forces of market capitalism and the working class (Olssen et al. 2004) (see Chapter 2). This compromise entailed 'natural rights, individualism and utilitarianism, property rights and human rights, liberalism and welfarism, capital and labour – a compromise which became increasingly embedded in economic policy' (O'Connor, 1984:201). In similar ways, that social democratic liberal policy diffused the revolutionary potential of the working class by allowing the state to mediate the functions of the market economy; the pedagogy encouraged in my example softened the worst excesses of a schooling that is, arguably, most concerned about creating a labour power suited to a market economy. This literacy, in marked contrast to more revolutionary forms of critical literacy, fails to challenge the deeper structures of schooling that ensures the continued cycles of social reproduction and inequality. For revolutionary critical literacy advocates, claims to neutrality in teaching are an impossibility (Freire 1985). If educators are not explicitly encouraging their students to see their reality as a problem, then they must be enabling them to accept it and adapt to it and thus engage in its reproduction (Allman 2001).

The pedagogy has embedded within it an implicit belief or assumption, or rhetoric of its political and ideological neutrality; the pleasures of engaging in the reading and writing of texts appear to reside outside of their place within the superstructure of society and have their own autonomy. From a post-structuralist position, the assumption that lies behind the forms of literacy teaching represented in my example are that the teaching is fulfilling the needs of the children (Giroux 1997). What is missing in the students are the 'culturally specific experiences that school authorities believe students must acquire in order to enrich the quality of their lives . . . underlying this view of experience is the logic of cultural deprivation theory that defines education in terms of cultural enrichment, remediation . . . .' (Giroux 1997:127). Giroux goes on to point out that what is offered as a form of privileged school experience is often an endorsement of a particular way of life. Life without the pleasures of reading and writing and the literate behaviors that form the substance of the school literacy experience could arguably be cast as 'other' or deviant in some way.

These last critical arguments derive from post-structuralist theoretical frames, many of which take the positions adopted by writers such as Janks. I discussed these writers earlier in this chapter and, as I have pointed out here and in Chapter 2, they have their own embedded conservative position which derives from their disillusionment with the possibilities for the destruction of the base of society – capitalism. Indeed, Marxists may argue that the forms of practice demonstrated by the pedagogy in my example privilege an autonomous literacy practice that may well represent the future of literacy teaching and curriculum after a revolution. As I have shown, Lenin approved of progressive education (Fitzpatrick 2002), and the influential progressive psychologist Lev Vygotsky was a Bolshevik. However, as part of a curriculum and pedagogy that is contained in the superstructures of a capitalist society it can only be deeply conservative in its impact. These pedagogies' left credentials are those of a reformist kind and constitute a continuation of the principles of social democratic liberalism in literacy teaching that has a long tradition in schooling.

Social Democratic Liberal Prescription: Concentrating on the Cognitive

I now want to turn to the work of educationalists (Mercer 2000, Mercer and Littleton 2007) who also seek to encourage empowering practice through their research and development projects, which, I want to argue, are influenced by social democratic liberal politics. However, there is a difference. The pedagogy I wish to describe now might be described as 'third way' (Giddens 2000) pedagogy, as it mixes explicit prescription with the rhetoric of democracy and arguably mirrors the 'third way' politics of Anthony Giddens and the New Labour government with its own compromises between democratic socialism and the liberalism (Blair 1998) that celebrates the market economy.

Ground Rules for Talk

Some of the most influential scholarship in the field of literacy and talk in classrooms over recent years have come from the work of Cambridge professor Neil Mercer and his colleagues (e.g., Mercer et al. 1999, Mercer 2000, Mercer and Littleton 2007) on introducing ground rules for talk in children's conversations in school. Mercer and his colleagues argue for encouraging what Mercer (2000) calls 'interthinking' between groups of children engaged in problem-solving activities. Interthinking describes the joint cognitive activity of those who solve problems together in a collaborative manner.

Interthinking as a concept derives from Vygotsky's notion of the zone of proximal development (ZPD), a state that occurs between teacher and student when the intramental (individual) processes are boosted by the intermental (social activity). Social learning, for Mercer, is in an 'intermental development zone (IDZ)' (2000:141) where learners draw on 'a more experienced other' and work as a group to think through problem solving activities. Ground rules for talk direct the forms of language use being applied in these situations to promote interthinking. Mercer and his colleagues have devised sets of teaching resources that have become very popular with teachers and educationalists (Cordon 2000, Grudgeon et al. 2001).

Mercer (2000) argues that in every conversation a mutual understanding is constructed between participants, creating the correct contexts for successful communication to occur. Through a set of mutually understood and sanctioned ground rules, which are applied to establish the nature of the language used within this context, these contexts will always be recreated in every new interaction that happens. These ground rules, according to Mercer, are the conventions that the participants in a conversation employ to make effective conversation possible. A shared understanding, manifested in the ground rules of talk that are applied, informs participants about what needs to be done to allow communication to occur.

The ground rules perspective contends that 'becoming an educated person' (Mercer and Littleton 2007:7) involves what are called 'special ways of using language'. Mercer and his colleagues propose that by introducing an agreed upon set of rules for talk for children to use in the classroom, opportunities for the children to work successfully on problem-solving activities will be assisted. Ground rules may appear as follows:

Our Ground Rules for Talk
We have agreed to:

Share ideas
Give reasons
Question ideas
Consider
Agree
Involve everybody
Everybody accepts responsibility.

Variations include:

1. We will talk together to think about what we do.
2. We will share what we know with each other.
3. We will ask everyone to say what they think.
4. Everyone will listen carefully to others and consider what we hear.
5. We will give reasons for what we say.
6. We will pay attention and try to think of good ideas.
7. We will decide what to do only when everyone has said all they want.
   (Dawes 2005:112)

Mercer and his colleagues (Mercer and Littleton 2007) are determined to show that ground rules for talk that are introduced in schools are done so democratically through careful negotiation between children and adults. Indeed, the ground rules perspective is often described by its proponents alongside arguments for democracy and fairness. Ground rules, like the ones shown above, create the context for reaching forms of discussion through what he describes as exploratory talk. This kind of talk occurs when the members of the group engage critically and constructively with each other. Ideas and statements are raised for challenge and counterchallenge, comments are always justified by those who make them and opinions are always sought from everybody. Mercer and Littleton (2007) describe this talk as being 'accountable' as it encourages everyone to challenge and to justify their views. Agreement is always the aim of discussion. 'It is a speech situation in which everyone is free to express their views and in which the most reasonable views gain acceptance' (Mercer and Littleton 2007:62). Mercer's contention is that exploratory talk 'embodies certain principles' (Mercer and Littleton 2007:66) of accountability which 'are highly valued in many societies particularly our own' (Mercer and Littleton 2007:66).

In previous articles (Lambirth 2006, 2009), I have challenged some of the claims for the implementation of ground rules for talk in classrooms as being not always as democratic as they appear. Some of the material available from the 'Thinking Together' (thinkingtogether.educ.cam.ac.uk/resources/downloads/preparing_for_group_work.pdf) teacher development resources, which is an example of one of the manifestations of Mercer's work available on the Web, suggests that teachers ask the children to devise rules for effective talk in the classroom. It then goes on to provide the teachers with the list of rules that have been seen to be effective and advices teachers to encourage the children to make up their own versions of these same rules. In effect, in this example, I have argued that it is a form of imposition and indeed prescription.

The research results that Mercer and his colleagues (Mercer et al., 1999 and Wegerif et al. 1999) show are very impressive. They describe how children who were involved in the 'Think Together' activities 'discussed issues in greater depth and for longer periods of time; participated more fully and equitably; more often sought justifications and provided reasons to support their views' (Mercer and Littleton 2007:84). The children's individual reasoning was tested by Raven's Progressive Matrices test (Raven et al. 1995) and it too showed that the children involved with ground rules in the thinking together sessions appeared to ' to have improved their individual nonverbal reasoning capabilities' (Mercer and Littleton 2007:85). Other further studies seem to confirm these results and the power of the ground rules model (Mercer et al. 2004, Dawes and Sams 2004).

I want to demonstrate a form of politically left critique of the work on ground rules. To do this, I first want to draw on the left post-structuralist perspectives of Fairclough (1992) who, I believe, would categorize the ground rules perspective as being part of an 'appropriateness model' of language variation. I then want to compare the underlying political principles behind the ground rules perspective with 'third way' social democratic liberal thought and policy.

Fairclough criticized classroom approaches that privileged an appropriateness model for teaching the norms of speech (Further education Unit 1987, DES 1988, 1989). The Cox report (DES 1989) was central to his criticism. It can be argued that the ground rules perspective attempts to construct the appropriate context within which conversations that resolve problems can occur. The idea about the need to create ground rules for talk in classrooms works at establishing that education should provide children with greater awareness and appreciation of 'functional language repertoire of the wider society and how it is used to create knowledge and carry out particular activities' (Mercer and Littleton 2007:68). It wants to define what is appropriate language use in these situations. Fairclough makes the argument that appropriateness models make misleading assumptions about socio-linguistic variation and he argues that such models come from confusion between sociolinguistic realities and political aspirations. He contends that:

In no actual speech community do all members always behave in accordance with a shared sense of which language varieties are appropriate for which contexts and purposes. Yet such a perfectly ordered world is set up as an ideal by those who wish to impose their own social order upon society in the realm of language. (1992:34)

Fairclough (1992) believes that appropriateness is an ideological category which is linked to partisan positions within the politics of language. Similar to ground rules for talk, appropriateness models make the claim that encouraging children to take up a new set of norms for their classroom talk will not mean they must give up other habitual ways of talking. Yet, in criticizing Cox, Fairclough asks 'how is it possible to add without replacing?' If one teaches children that a specific form of talk is better and more prestigious and powerful in contexts like schools, universities and other formal arenas for discussion, it makes children's own habitual ways of talking rather marginal and irrelevant. This, it can be argued, is an attack on the language use and identity of subordinated groups and may contribute to forms of alienation in children's perception of school which maintain the consistent patterns of underachievement, social reproduction and inequality.

Fairclough goes so far as to argue that language standardization is a form of class hegemony and an extension into the cultural domains of contestations and struggle between class and other groups. Fairclough contends that seemingly neat hegemonic attachments of language variety to particular contexts and purposes is nothing less than the political objectives of the dominate sections of society. The links that are made in appropriateness models, like ground rules, Fairclough would argue, have never been a socio-linguistic reality.

Using the principles behind these arguments, Mercer's methodological stance and approach are focused on the cognitive effects of the interventions he prescribes and are presented as ideologically neutral. There is little consideration or interest in the political and socio-economic dimensions of his work and therefore the results of his studies cannot show the other more socio-cultural and political results of schooling which presents children with the 'right' ways to speak.

Third Way Compromise

In Fairclough's critique of appropriate models of language use, he argues that if the teaching of standard English spoken grammars can be associated with the 'old right' in politics (Barnes 1988, Fairclough 1992) then the teaching of prescribed language competences and skills is typical of the politics of the modernizing new right associated with New Labour in the United Kingdom and the successive government formed by the Conservative Party. I want to pursue this a little here in the context of ground rules

for talk and a discussion on 'third way' politics that was very influential on
the policy of New Labour politicians (Blair 1998).

Giddens (2000) described the 'third way' as a means to reconfiguring
social democratic liberal doctrines in response to globalization and the
advent of the knowledge economy. New Labour's leader in the United
Kingdom, Tony Blair (1998), also saw the third way's potential for essential
compromise. He constructed a vision combining the classical liberalism
that asserted the primacy of individual liberty and the market economy with
social democratic liberalism, which advocated the need for social justice.
For both Giddens and Blair, there was a recognition that the government
and the state had an essential role to play in maintaining a prosperous
market economy. One could argue that third way politics hoped to unite
the two classic warring factions of the middle class – those who supported
state intervention and those who supported the supremacy of the market.
In turn, for education, it was an attempt to make alliances between those
supporters of visible pedagogy with those who advocated the more social
democratic liberal invisible pedagogies that I have discussed.

In broader political terms, the third way wanted a flourishing market
economy with strong social cohesion. Two precepts acted as the foundation
to these objectives: no rights without responsibilities and no authority
without democracy (Giddens 1998: 64–8). Giddens also argues for a replacement of the social democratic liberal call for 'egalitarianism at all costs'
(Giddens 2000: 85–86) with what he calls a 'dynamic life chances approach',
a policy that places the stress on equality of opportunity for all even if this
means that larger inequalities still persisted (Olssen et al. 2004).

I want to argue that educational literacy practice like those advocated
by Mercer and his colleagues can be located within this political and
ideological frame. The ground rules perspectives offers a compromise
between visible and invisible pedagogies – the pedagogies advocated by two
significant and powerful factions of middle class society (Bernstein 1996).
It offers a relaxation of hierarchical (regulative) rules in the way it claims
to present the ground rules for talk as a co-constructed framework for
language to be used by children in discussion, while maintaining strong
criterial rules in its insurance that specific forms of speech deemed to be
'correct' in official contexts are taught to the children. Once the right
ways of putting forward argument are found, then an equality of opportunity is provided by this new model that affects change in an empowering
way. Here, as in the conservative pedagogy described in Chapter 5, there is
a robust positivist self-assurance in the content of the curriculum, typical of
neoliberal approaches to education. Yet it is coupled with a declared desire
to include values and subjectivity within the mix of their perspectives

which gives it a flavour of social justice and the recognition of the need to recognize and foster an understanding about the known inequalities in society and the importance of socio-cultural subjectivities in its paradigm.

The ground rules perspective provides arguments for its pedagogy's emancipatory potential while making claims for ensuring the accountability of those in discussion. From these principles one can see, operating within a left Marxist framework, that within a capitalist economy which forms the base of society, children are being offered the means to use language as 'educated people' do, and so are offered levels of power to operate in society. This approach also makes available new forms of labour power and so operates upon a 'planning perspective' and the new requirements for employees in a changing capitalist economy. Fairclough contends:

> It is orientated to a new conception of citizenship, and sense that modes of hegemony must change in a rapidly changing world . . . what appropriateness hopes to do . . . is effect compromise between these Old Right and New Right perspectives and priorities. It is the linchpin which holds them together in an uneasy, and no doubt temporary harmony. (1992:43)

It is these forms of compromise in broad political terms which, I want to argue, have helped create so much popularity for this kind of approach to the teaching of talk. As I have mentioned earlier in my discussion of other forms of literacy practice influenced by social democratic liberal ideals, critique of these methods from a Marxist left position, allows the opportunity to recognize their potential after the demise of the present base of society – capitalism. As I discussed in Chapter 1, many Marxists recognize some autonomy in culture and literacy and perceive that the most powerful and rich literacy practices are at present used and guarded by the ruling class. This would include the forms of language advocated by Mercer and others. Yet, Marxists may also recognize that education within capitalism can use pedagogy as a weapon against the working class and other subordinated groups in the way this book describes.

In this chapter, I have offered examples of social democratic liberal practices that are often seen as operating within more left political perspectives and have shown that from a more radical left and Marxist perspective they remain fundamentally conservative. I have attempted to show how much of this practice is based around a myth of neutrality, but that much of the politics is set firmly within a class context. In the next chapter, I will discuss the practice associated with radical critical literacy perspectives. This approach, too, will be subjected to critique as we continue our journey through methods that might be called literacy of the left.

Chapter 7

Radical Discourse and Literacy Practice

In this chapter, I want to explore what has been called revolutionary critical education (Allman 2001, McLaren and Jaramillo 2007), exploring its philosophy and practices. I will begin with a brief discussion of the work of the Brazilian educator Paulo Freire – perhaps one of the most famous exponents of critical literacy pedagogy – setting out the context within which he formed his ideas and the nature of his educational project. This cannot be a comprehensive description and discussion of his work, but I hope it will be enough to position him within quadrant 3. I will then present the work of some of those who have championed his legacy, as well as those who have argued strongly against the postmodernist left's social democratic liberal interpretations of Freire's work, which, arguably, corrupt the essential revolutionary nature of his writings. Throughout, I will offer a critique of Freire and his followers' positions from a classic Marxist perspective, with the charge that many of the ideas of revolutionary critical literacy advocates take an idealistic and overly moralistic approach and sideline Marxism's materialist conception of history. In doing so, it could be argued that they are themselves open to charges of reformist tendencies and fail to offer a realistic perspective for teachers and educators working in schools and colleges today.

Paulo Freire

Freire was born in Brazil in 1921 to middle class parents. His childhood corresponded with economic depression and despite his petit bourgeois background he shared experiences of hunger and poverty with others in the country, but, as he has commented (Mackie 1980:3), he shared the poverty 'not the class'. Freire went on to study at Recife University where he eventually was made professor of history and philosophy of education in 1959. Preceding this, Freire was a teacher, along with his wife, and was active in the Catholic Action Movement. It was then that he began to form his political perspectives and 'decided not to keep working with the bourgeois, and instead to work with the people' (quoted in Mackie 1980:3). In 1962, Freire was appointed coordinator of an adult literacy programme in Brazil and it was as part of this project that he devised his famous 'culture circles'. His work and influence grew, but with it came criticism from the Brazilian right-wing media that his work was subversive and grounded in Communist ideals. In 1964, a military coup toppled the Goulart government and Freire was arrested, removed from his job and imprisoned for 75 days. Eventually Freire was granted political asylum in Bolivia, but later had to leave for Chile after a coup in Bolivia meant that Friere would be no longer safe. In Chile, he became involved in the Agrarian Reform Corporation that put an adult literacy programme into action. Freire went on to be given a chair at Harvard University and in 1970 took up an appointment as a special consultant to the Office of Education at the World Council of Churches in Geneva.

Praxis

The point has been made (Allman 2001) that as crucial to understanding Freire, one must recognize that everything he wrote also concerned the role of revolutionary leadership and how the leader must work and learn alongside the people. Indeed, all his work on education unites the role of revolutionary with that of teacher in the essential need to create dialogue between those who teach or lead with the people. Freire wished to 'defend the eminently pedagogical character of the revolution' (1996:49). Like revolutionaries, the teachers must have a profound trust in their students:

> Through dialogue, the teacher-of-the-students and students-of-the-teacher cease to exist and a new term emerges: teacher-student with student-teachers. The teacher is no longer merely the-one-who-teaches, but one who is himself taught in dialogue with the students, who in turn while being taught also teaches. (Freire 1996:61)

Through articulation of this form of relationship, Freire shows his deep belief that revolution is a process with an essential educational component and, equally, he believed that education is a political process. For him, education will either domesticate people or aim to contribute to their liberation through encouraging the people to liberate themselves. Therefore, educators responsible for teaching others must make the political decision between liberation or domestication (Allman 2001). Freire writes that, 'conversion to the people requires a profound rebirth. Those who undergo it must take on a new form of existence; they can no longer remain as they were' (1996: 43). This is an important part of Freire's attitude to revolutionary change and, with the assistance of another commentator (Walker 1980), later in this chapter, I want to critique this position as a flaw in Freire's relationship with Marxism.

Freire's approach to perceiving education as either liberating of domesticating is reflected in Gramci's famous words about literacy: that it is a 'two edged sword. It can be repressive or liberating'. All of his work sought to use critical literacy education as a way to free those he taught. During his literacy projects in Brazil, Freire and his colleagues set up 'culture circles' within the villages and the slums where he worked. The culture circles encouraged debate and dialogue between the students and the teachers, which would attempt to clarify situations and seek action from the clarification that would arise (Freire 1976). The discussions ranged across a wide list of topics that included nationalism, the vote and democracy. It was these discussions that formed Freire's conviction about how he should approach literacy teaching. Learning to read, for example, must be a process where the actual content and material of the learning must be directly relevant to the students' daily life and problems. This would contribute to a change in consciousness of their everyday political, social and cultural environment (Bee 1985). 'A critical perception of reality enables people to know what needs changing . . . further more it is this perception of reality that creates the will or the motivation in people to risk themselves in revolutionary struggle' (Allman 2001:93). Here, typical to Freire's revolutionary critical literacy, revolution is integral to the objectives of the pedagogy. The chief object of the process of learning literacy was not one of merely mastering the technical aspects of using the written word, but a quality of consciousness which would establish within the students a changed awareness that could be expressed through language and action.

Freire, while working with peasant students in Brazil, found that he needed to convince them of their own worth and that despite the poverty they were in they had the power to be the movers and makers of history. The significance of the power of the spoken and written word in finding this awareness and belief became central to Freire's work with his students. Its centrality revolved, however, in how the written word can be utilized by the oppressed classes as a tool for revolution in its traditional forms.

As I discussed in Chapter 3, 'revolutionary critical literacy' (Allman 2001), in contrast to more post-structuralist left manifestations of literacy practices, sees the learning of 'standard' language structures as crucial for the political empowerment of their students, yet this technical mastery of the language is placed in the context of ways with words that contribute to revolutionary struggle. Chris Searle, a practitioner of this form of approach to critical literacy, is clear about the importance of using language 'correctly':

> Critical literacy can only be credible pedagogy if it extends and enlarges the powers of language of the students and gives them the opportunity and ability to be in full control of the all the words they need. This means an understanding of basic grammar and sentence analysis, the power to spell correctly and use punctuation effectively, to know the figures of speech and write sequentially and coolly. (1998:13)

The power to manipulate language for Searle, as it was for Freire, was crucial to how they saw language as a weapon and a tool that could be used by the working class and peasants to change society. Here an autonomous model of literacy emerges and creates a clear distinction as it is being influenced by Marxism. Standard language use, although recognized as being an ideological weapon used upon the subordinated class to differentiate, discriminate and 'other' (see 'Introduction'), is also conceptualized here as being an autonomous weapon that can be turned on its owners – the ruling class - and manipulated for subversive and liberating ends.

Freire also argues that psychologically and mechanically possessing reading and writing techniques is not enough either. They must possess and use these techniques 'in terms of consciousness to understand what is read, what is written and why one writes' (Bee 1980:43). For this to happen, like the revolutionary, the educator must enter into a dialogue with the students about real situations – this is praxis. Praxis is a term borrowed from Marx:

> ... circumstances are changed by men and that the educator must himself be educated. This doctrine must, therefore, divide society into two parts, one of which is superior to society. The coincidence of the changing of circumstances and of human activity or self-change can be conceived and rationally understood only as revolutionary praxis. ([1845]1975, CW5:4)

Marx's development of the term praxis can be traced back. The materialism of the French Enlightenment had used empiricism to emphasize experience as the source of all thinking and that our whole consciousness and

essence derives from the situation within which one has been placed. This
materialist approach led to the doctrine that emphasized the need to transform the state in order to make it more conducive for the development of
human beings. Marx argued from this that if man is shaped by his environment, his whole environment must be made more human ([1845]1975:
131). Robert Owen ([1812]1970) also drew on this perspective to argue
that the notion that people were responsible for their own character was
false. Owen believed that the most important way to form peaceful, responsible minds was through the formation of character by education. Indeed,
these ideas were fundamental to reformist agendas which made education
central to improving society. But Marx asks the question 'Who is the educator?' The theoretical component of this form of materialism does not
take this question into account. For Marx, this form of materialism divides
society into two parts, one of which is raised above the other. The source of
the educational intervention which is suggested resides within the social
totality. Marx's position was an appeal to educators who were 'enlightened
rulers or to some class privileged in insight and wisdom. In the context of
the materialist theory, such moves could hardly amount to more than the
introduction of a *deus ex machina* to solve the problem' (Small 2005:38).
Marx's answer to this was his theory of revolutionary praxis which Freire
draws on in his writings.

Praxis for Marx was a mode of human activity within the human world
(Small 2005). It involves the changing not only of the object, but the agent as
well. Marx describes how in revolution the changing of oneself coincides with
the changing of circumstances. In effect, the influences with which circumstances have upon the individual involved becomes part of the activity. Using
Marx's dialectical position, the materialist perspective, as discussed earlier, is
one-sided in nature. One side is the only active agent. For Marx, in any social
interaction all the parties are active agents who act in ways which will determine the outcomes of the specific activity with which they engage. Acting and
being acted upon go together. However, not all action is praxis, and a vital
component in this exchange of actions is a critical element. As Small explains:
'The role of consciousness is not the role of spectator or onlooker. It is bound
up with evaluation, choice, decision, because it is in these processes that the
unity of theory and practice can be achieved' (2005:42).

Freire was sure that if the learner is made into a passive object by the
process of education then they are also made dependent and mute in the
face of what is perceived to be superior knowledge. The only way to break
away from this is through a form of praxis: reflection and action upon the
world with a view to transform it. True reflection has to include action.

Freire's pedagogy must include concomitant involvement with dialogue and communication at its core.

> The task of the educator is to present the subject as a problem, the content of which mediates it and not to discourse on it, extend it or hand it over, as if it were matter of something already done, constituted, completed, finished. In this process no one can present something to someone else as a problem, while at the same time remaining a spectator. (Connolly 1980:72)

Schooling for Changing Consciousness: A Short Critique

Marx's definition of class included a dynamic element (McLellan 1980). A class must be conscious of itself and carry a common hostility to the social group by which it is dominated. This perspective, arguably, is reflected in Freire's view that 'it is only when the oppressed find the oppressor out and become involved in the organized struggle for their liberation that they begin the believe in themselves' (Freire 1996:47). Marx argued that as part of its defining characteristic, a class must be organized politically to fight for its own interests (Marx [1845–46]1974). Individuals belong to a class in so far as that they carry this common cause of hostility against another class. The consciousness of individuals to recognize their membership of a class is vital. The consequence of not acting together would lead to hostility and competition against one another, as worker vies with other workers in competition over the sale of their labour power. According to Marx, the struggle between the bourgeoisie and proletariat over surplus value (see Chapter 1) only becomes political when they become 'a class for itself' (Marx [1845–46]1974:48). Before this level of class-consciousness and class antagonism, they remain a theoretical 'class in opposition' (Marx [1845–46]1974:48).

Yet, Marx never advocated schools as being the centres for the development of this class-consciousness. Like Freire's perspectives, Marx recognized the importance of developing class-consciousness while embedded within the contexts of capitalist oppression. However, schools may not be the best place for this raising of the consciousness to occur. Marx wrote: 'Trade Unions are the schools of socialism. It is in trade unions that workers educate themselves and become socialists because under their very eyes and everyday the struggle with capital is taking place' (1869). Obviously, Freire was working with rural peasants and therefore the context for struggle was very different, but in 1871, Marx declared that, instead of trade unions the political party was the only way the workers could organize themselves to fight against the collective powers of the possessing classes. Indeed, the concept of the vanguard party as a means to educate and develop class consciousness has been the favoured means to organize for revolution (Trotsky 1932, Cannon 1967). Trotsky contended that 'the proletariat found its weapon in Marxism' (1980:51) and its description of class society and its antagonisms, as a means of transforming society. In addition, Marxism as a theory potentially facilitates crucial levels of class-consciousness in those who read and understand it (Lambirth 2010). In organizations that are created solely for class demands a praxis is more likely to occur as leadership by those directly involved in the struggle means motivations are channelled and objectives are clear. Freire's demand that teachers must be 're-born' and develop a new form of existence is needed less when all those who are directly acting and leading the struggle are themselves those that desire the change. Schooling's role in revolution from this perspective is of less significance when the oppressed control other political structures within which to affect change.

Walker (1980) criticizes Freire for the way he interprets Marx and his belief in the ability of the petit bourgeois to create the spark for revolution through their leadership and education by critical literacy pedagogy. In his critique of Freire, Walker is sensitive to Freire's relationship with his religious faith. He points out that Freire's Christianity always influenced his approach to emancipatory action. In a famous quote, Freire (1974) explains his combination of both Christianity with Marxism:

> When I was a young man, I went to the people, to the workers, the peasants, motivated, really, by my Christian faith . . . . I talked with the people, I learned to speak with the people – the pronunciation, the words, the concepts. When I arrived with the people – the misery, the concreteness, you know! But also the beauty of the people, the openness, the ability to love which the people have the friendship . . ..
>
> The obstacles of this reality sent me – to Marx. I started reading and studying. It was beautiful because I found in Marx a lot of things the people had told me – without being literate. Marx was a real genius.
>
> But when I met Marx, I continued to meet Christ on the corners of the street – by meeting the people

Walker (1980) argues that this quote reveals Freire's relationship with both Christianity and Marxism and that Freire's political method and social thought was under the greater influence of Christianity. This is demonstrated, he argues, by Freire's involvement with the World Council of Churches.

For Walker, Christian thinking is central in Freire's discussions around praxis and the role of the educator and the change he or she must undergo. This change is described by Freire as a form of Easter experience. Leaders 'must die as elitist so as to be resurrected on the side of the oppressed, that they are born again with the beings who are allowed to be' (Freire 1973:2). Walker (1980) describes how for Freire, leadership in revolution must inevitably be petit bourgeois in character. The Easter experience of renouncing one's own class in favour of another as Freire describes it is voluntary and consists of an 'extraordinary moral commitment and sacrifice' (Walker 1980:135). It makes the ideas, consciousness and moral consistency of the bourgeois absolutely crucial if the transformation of society is to succeed. It is here that Walker contends that Freire ignores some basic tenets of Marxism and allows his Christianity to control his thinking.

> It is the expression of his fundamental existentialist-Christian orienta-
> tion, in this case the idea of a specially sanctioned, self-sacrificial mission-
> ary role for the educator leaders . . . . Even supposing that it is realistic to
> preach such a gospel, supposing that the 'sacrificial missionary' class will
> respond or even that it is possible to respond, it is a further question
> whether the response will have the political effects expected of it, namely
> that *sui generic* moral will cancel out class conflict. (Walker 1980:136)

As Walker points out, Marx was certain that a classless society could only be achieved through the action of the working class by acting for itself. It may be true that certain historical moments in this struggle may see the petit bourgeoisie united in their interests with the working class, but the working class would be wise to abstain from being led by this other class as the nature of class struggle means betrayal would be the most familiar occurrence. For Marx, events may proletarianize the petit bourgeoisie, but it will only be events that can do this in any revolutionary way. That, for Marx, is how changes in consciousness for emancipatory transformation can occur. Attempts to change consciousness through schooling and independently of developments in the base of society are, according to Walker, idealistic and utopian and are a misunderstanding of Marx's analysis of how society develops and can be transformed.

Moulding Consciousness for Socialism

Interesting recent research (Kane 2007) produced data on 278 members of the Scottish Socialist Party in the United Kingdom and their perception of

'the educational influences responsible for shaping their identity as politically radical active citizens' (Kane 2007:72). As Kane describes, there is
plenty of research available on radical 'adult popular education' that attempts
to speculate on the most effective practices that enable the oppressed of the
world 'to overcome naïve passivity and become critically aware "subjects for
social change"' (p. 54). In Kane's research, he starts with the activists themselves, those who are already critically aware, and works backwards through
their life histories to explore the educational experiences, both formal and
informal, that shaped their consciousness in this way.

Kane's data was generated in the form of answers from questionnaires
and, although he finds ambiguity about the meaning of some of the results,
clear patterns appeared to emerge. An important role was found to reside
in formal education, for example, primary school was thought to be a factor. He found that non-formal (as opposed to in-formal) adult education
was almost unanimously considered as playing a positive part in the formation of their perspectives. However, compared to other categories like
events, personality traits and family, this kind of education's overall influence was low. 'By contrast, the adult education taking place informally
within the categories of 'political party' and 'industrial disputes, political
demonstrations and local or single-issue campaigns ranked among the most
important influences' (Kane 2007:72). This appears to be an example of
how a number of factors can be influential in changing the consciousness
of those that become Socialists/Marxists, but a powerful factor still appears
to be those that Marx, Lenin, and Trotsky also perceived as being so, namely
events and action within the traditional organizations of the working class.
Education either formal or non-formal is clearly influential, but lags behind
the power of events and this is supported by other research (Bennet 1999,
Benn 2000).

Modern Theoretical Manifestations of
Revolutionary Critical Literacy Pedagogy

A great deal of critical literacy education praises the work of Paulo Freire, as
we saw in Chapter 6, yet much of it takes a reformist position, often not con-
sidering the transformative possibilities of some of critical literacy's manifestations. McLaren and Jaramillo (2007) have highlighted this in their
passionate demand for revolutionary critical pedagogy. Instead of only
denouncing the injustices of 'neo-liberal capitalism, critiquing the current
global crisis of over-production, stagnation, and environmental ruin' (p. 94)
they wish to use these forms of pedagogy to construct means to rid the world

of it forever. This would include critical literacy practices. McLaren and Jaramillo make their readers aware of how critical literacy practice often aims to seek social justice in society, but that this term 'all too frequently operates to cover for legitimizing capitalism' (p. 94) or for their belief in its intractability. They go on to write:

> The critical tradition in education has become irrevocably alienated from its Marxist roots, and has undergone a disparaging rejection of the insurrectionary energies of critical theorists since energies have, over the years, become suffused with the accelerated transformation of a bipolar cold war politics into unilateral domination by the United States. (McLaren and Jaramillo 2007:84)

McLaren and Jaramillo perceive this to be also the fault of the 'embourgeoisement' of critical pedagogy, which has failed to recognize the class nature of U S culture and now has perceived superiority in bourgeois thought and subjectivity.

Lack of Revolutionary Teaching Practice

In the last chapter (Chapter 6), I categorized forms of critical pedagogy based around post-structuralism as being part of a social democratic liberal discourse. Much of it does not desire to create a synergy between education and revolution and is happy to settle for social justice within the existing economic system. Yet there are plenty of examples of practice based around these perspectives (Larson and Marsh 2005, Janks 2010) which demonstrate its practical manifestation.

The latest work by Janks (2010) is a good example of critical literacy based around a post-structuralist theoretical frame and offers vignettes of how this theory can feed into practice in schools around the world, including in Janks' native South Africa. Janks (2010) provides her readers with her own orientation to critical literacy. She describes how different 'conceptualisations of the relationship between language and power' (p. 23) 'foregrounds one or other of: domination, access, diversity or design' (p. 23). Domination she describes as the way theorists view language and other symbolic forms and discourse as a means of maintaining and reproducing relations of domination. As I have already discussed in Chapter 6, power is given no central source, as it is by Marxists, within this perspective. Power in Janks' model is opaque, dispersed and varied. For Janks' description of access, she offers what Janks (2004) has called the 'access paradox'. Access to powerful language forms presents a paradox that says 'how can one provide children with access to powerful language and discourse, while at the same time valuing and promoting the diverse literacies that many children bring into school from home?' By providing the access it perpetuates their dominance, while if children are denied access there is a danger of marginalizing children from the society that values these powerful language forms. Of course, continuing the Marxist critique, this paradox becomes unimportant when the critical literacy and informal educational practices outside of school are aimed at developing a revolution which will destroy the source of power that manufacture these elite forms of language use – the ruling class – and enable the working class to expropriate these forms for themselves in a truly democratic society. Janks' paradox itself reveals her social democratic liberal left account of power and arguably the inability of her theorizing to see past this paradox which arguably exists, if one takes a Marxist line, because of the superstructures that surround capitalism (see Chapter 1).

For Janks, diversity looks at how the different ways of reading and writing around the world are undertaken in a range of modalities. Diversity of language is embedded and informed by the 'wide range of social identities' (p. 25) found in diverse social institutions. This creates the need to reflect on these communicative repertoires practiced in different social fields. This too, from a Marxist perspective, fails to understand the nature of super-structures that exist around capitalism (Chapter 1) and is misguided in the way she appears to believe that some genuine form of class 'ownership' of the diversity of forms of literacy can be credited to oppressed groups and not to the construction of social superstructures by capitalist means of production and exchange.

Janks' conception of design is encompassed within the idea of productive power. This form of power brings the ability to draw on 'a multiplicity of semiotic systems across diverse cultural locations to challenge and change existing discourses' (2010:25). Janks argues that concentrating on only one of these aspects of literacy – domination, diversity, access and design – creates an imbalance. Janks argues that 'we need to find ways of holding all these elements in productive tension to achieve what is a shared goal for all critical literacy work; equity and social justice' (2010:27).

Already, those who have taken in the different arguments on the left found in this book will be able to analyse the political traditions that Janks' work rests upon. The noble shared goals that this work arguably aims towards, would be criticized by commentators like McLaren and Jaramillo (2007), as being a social democratic liberal compromise. The literacy work aims to improve circumstances within the existing socio-economic structures within society. It takes a moral position for more equity and justice. These, as we have seen, are central to social democratic liberal reformist tendencies. As a consequence, it can be described as being fundamentally conservative in nature. Its failure to include in the pedagogy, direct links with revolution; its silence on the need for practitioners to cross barriers and reach out to the people and commit 'class suicide' (Freire 1996, Walker 1980); the absence of recognition or condemnation of a central source of power – capitalism – means that Janks' literacy pedagogy proposals cannot, from a more radical left perspective, reside in the same quadrant of my literacy pedagogy typology. Therefore Janks' claim to advocate a form of 'critical literacy' begins to become questionable.

Janks (2010) provides interesting vignettes of the work she and other colleagues have been undertaking with students that demonstrate how the four areas of critical literacy can be united within the pedagogy. In one example, she describes what she calls the 'dominant deconstruction' of an advertisement for Edge Razors (Janks 2010:28). The advertisement provided multimodal representations and the student group of secondary school learners used all four of these 'knowledges as lenses' (Janks 2010:29). As a result of these discussions and then later proceeding to design their own advertisements, the students began to be able to unpick the issues around these posters. Issues concerning the negative construction of women were discussed alongside an understanding of how different values from different cultures were ignored by the advertising agency designers, but they also discussed how decisions in these forms of design will often exclude many. In conclusion, Janks describes how the students had a 'much greater awareness of the relationship between domination, diversity and design'. Yet, the absence and silence concerning the source of the domination, levels of access and the political nature of diversity and design are never given a clear focus as it would inevitably have been in more revolutionary left critical pedagogies. Marxists may well want to argue that this form of teaching presents a politically 'safe' model, typical of what Bernstein (1996) would describe as middle class progressive techniques which, he would argue, lead to a continuation of social reproductive patterns. Moral foundations to pedagogy, however, can be found in other forms of radical and Marxist positions.

Marxist Moral Positions?

As I have already described, McLaren and Jaramillo (2007) argue determinedly against liberal reformers. They argue that long-term reform is not possible and that we cannot make capitalism more humane. Their pedagogy is fixed on teachers using education to allow the working class to discover how they are exploited and to use schooling as Allman (2001) describes to 'critique the existing conditions, a counter hegemonic project' (p. 120). Yet, McLaren and Jaramillo (2007) may be accused of forgetting the objective and scientific analysis that Marx made concerning how human society has developed and will do so in the future. They can be accused of striking a moral note in some of their writing concerning the injustices of capitalism. On pages 82–83 of their book McLaren and Jaramillo (2007) passionately list the injustices and immorality that capitalism brings to the poor and oppressed and argue the impossibility of capitalism being made more humane. They stress what they call the 'absurdity' of capital and that it violates the requirements of justice.

There are Marxists (Woods 2008) who would accuse this approach of being 'utopian', a perspective that sees the advent of socialism as a moral imperative. Marx argued that socialism must have a material basis and could only manifest itself through the development of productive forces under capitalism. It is only when capitalism is unable to offer workers any hope of prosperity, will they, by drawing on the organs of the labour movement, carry out their historical mission to overthrow the system and create a classless society. Marx took capitalism to be an essential period in the development of human society. He was aware of its brutality and its oppressive forces, but, ultimately, it has been responsible for not only the expansion of human ingenuity in science and the arts, but also has grown the seeds of its own demise most significantly by the development of an organized working class. As I described in Chapter 1, for Marxism, every new crisis in the capitalist economy brings with it the need for the working class to change society. Marx also saw the superficiality of reform of the conditions of the working class, but was adamant that only the working class could change society forever. It would not be education through schooling that would make this happen but events brought about by economic crisis. McLaren and Jarmillo (2007), arguably, are too determined to challenge the immoral nature of ideas of neoliberal capitalism through schooling and forms of critical pedagogy and they lose sight of one of the basic tenets of Marxism: its is only through struggle that ideas will change. It is this with which I wish to conclude this chapter.

Beyond Critical Pedagogy

As I have shown, there are many examples of these forms of post-structuralist literacy pedagogies available for analysis. However, Hatcher (2007) argues that, in contrast, there are almost no modern practical manifestations of revolutionary critical pedagogy of the type advocated by Freire (1996), Searle (1998) or McLaren and Jarmillo (2007) to be found in either the United States or the United Kingdom. Hatcher speculates that this may be because of levels of surveillance of teachers in classrooms from government agencies, or, more important, that teachers themselves are simply not interested in teaching in the way Marxist Revolutionary pedagogues suggest that they do. In Chapter 3, I described the work of Chris Searle and his form of practice, which I consider most akin to the revolutionary praxis encouraged by Freire. The absence of modern models may suggest that these ideas have little effect in schools and that other ways to change the consciousness of the youth need to be found, if indeed this form of educational objective is what is required.

As Hatcher (2007) describes, the consistent presence of trade unions, political parties and campaigning associations offer more hope. Hatcher holds that it is in the context of action that socialist and Marxist ideas have the greatest purchase, not just on a small minority of individuals but on a whole culture. This idea was supported by the research undertaken by Kane (2007) that I discussed earlier.

The most powerful work in left education for Hatcher (2007) happens collectively in organized groups. In education, teacher trade unions and education associations like The United Kingdom Literacy Association or The National Association of English Teachers in the United Kingdom. For Hatcher they provide:

- Hospitable networks to discuss educational policy and if need be how to act against it.
- Action around the SATS, academies, privatization and teachers pay and conditions could be organized around these groups.
- They can create opportunities for the consciousness of teachers to change through action against attacks on the common principles of those working in education.
- For students in youth groups of political parties and other political youth organizations.

Hatcher offers a different perspective on the notion of left teachers and how they can influence change. This position throws doubt on the role of education of any kind to be the main catalyst for change in society. Instead, teachers working and campaigning together to improve conditions through associations and trade unions offers them another source of power.

It combines solidarity between groups of workers with an awareness of the importance of events and movements in society in general as a way to seek transformative actions. The next chapter considers this in more detail.

In this chapter, I introduced the ideas of Paulo Freire as perhaps the most famous theorist and exponent of revolutionary critical pedagogy. His dedication and determination to creating an explosive synergy between education and revolution puts him and his many followers into quadrant 3 of my literacy pedagogy typology. I critiqued his work from a classic Marxist perspective, beginning to question the wisdom of choosing schooling as a way of encouraging a class consciousness in the working class and other oppressed groups. I contrasted revolutionary praxis with the work of a leading critical literacy pedagogue from the post-structuralist tradition and concluded with the work of Richard Hatcher and his strategy for education and social change. Hatcher's view appears to be in the traditions of more classic Marxist positions and, in the 'Conclusions', I consider the theory and practice of education from classic Marxist perspectives.

Chapter 8

Marxist Discourse and Literacy Practice

This chapter is dedicated to classic Marxist perspectives on literacy education. It builds on Chapter 1 of this book and much of what has already been said throughout about Marxism and its account of literacy and schooling. The practice that I want to describe in this chapter is found in quadrant 4 of my typology of literacy pedagogy. The models of teaching literacy and education here are different than those shown in the other quadrants. This is because Marx unequivocally saw education as being controlled by the class that owns the means of production. Marx's materialist conception of history (see Chapter 1) describes how changes in the modes of production inevitably lead to the need for education to change with them. Hence, the nature of education's development over history, which has been mediated by the economic and social base of society and society's specific needs. Consequently, the ability for schooling in any one epoch to prepare pupils for another is problematic, as Marx envisaged the need for a revolutionary period in order to make the transition. This problem has led to a great deal of controversy among Marxist scholars and revolutionaries about what exactly can be done in school and elsewhere to prepare for change. As we have seen, left literacy practice wishes to make an impact, either on the individual student or between groups of students, changing the consciousness of those being educated for equitable purposes. So, from a Marxist perspective how can this be best achieved? In this chapter, I will describe what Marx has said about schooling within capitalism that hints at future education after a revolution. To do so, I will briefly describe the work of Robert Owen in the nineteenth century and then Marx's conception of polytechnic education. I will go on to introduce classic Marxist revolutionary views about education outside of school and its capability to prepare workers for revolutionary transition, with particular concentration on the role of the vanguard party for education and class consciousness and the efforts of workers' organizations in schooling their own class. This will lead to a discussion about post-revolutionary Russia and its experience at creating socialist education. Finally, I shall attempt to sum up some of the controversy concerning Marxism and education that exists between modern scholars in the field.

Marxism and Education

In 'Introduction', I showed the derivation of the concept of a 'left' in politics. One of these sources came from the formation of the left Hegelians, of which Marx was a member. It is mainly because of this that Marx and Marxism has played such a central role in this book, representing one extreme of left thinking about literacy and education. Marx fundamentally believed that one's social consciousness was a product of the economic and social conditions in which we find ourselves. However, Marx was also clear that there is a dialectical relationship between the two and that social conscious can also shape the social and economic conditions of societies. Education, in some form or other, has a crucial role to play:

> Education is the name we give to the planned and systematic shaping of consciousness. Socialists have always understood the importance of education as an instrument of social transformation, and have given it great priority in their strategies. (Castles and Wustenburg 1979:1)

As I discussed in Introduction, the history of education can be retold from a social class position (Hill 2001, Cole 2006, Ball 2008). In Chapter 1, I showed how this class perspective is reflected in Marxism's conception of human society as evolving and developing by means of a series of epoch-changing revolutions. Our own conception of modernity has been sculpted by Britain's industrial revolution and the rise of the modern bourgeoisie based around the power of financial capital. For Marx, when one mode of production has reached the limits of its own expansion and can no longer resist the challenge from the new rising social class, a new mode of production can begin. The transitions that occurred when feudalism was replaced by capitalism and when capitalism will be replaced by socialism are periods of crisis and revolution. Marx contended, through his materialist conception of history, that these changes in the base of society and the mode of production that formed this base also established changes in the social and political structures – the superstructures of one society. Education in the old society inevitably makes way for the education needed to support the new. Marx was clear that education is controlled by the ruling class whose actions are designed to support the modes of production that form the base of society. Within this society, education or schooling can provide the general capabilities and the training necessary for vocations specifically attuned for a particular class which supports the base of society. The second function of an education system is to pass on religious and political ideology which justifies the existing form of class domination.

Literacy education is central to these class-orientated objectives for education in each epoch. For some Marxists (Castle and Wustenburg 1979), the main aim for the ruling class concerning those from the lower classes is to prevent them from perceiving the structures and functions of society as they really are. This is often achieved by making this learning abstract and compartmentalized in order to maximize efficiency for when members of the lower classes meet their specific jobs. Criticality is avoided in favour of basic skills training. Many on the left (as we have seen in previous chapters) have argued that education for freedom means avoiding specialization and instead demanding good-quality scientific, political and cultural education for all. Yet, how can this be achieved in a society essentially dominated by a ruling class? Later in this chapter, I shall discuss the views of Marxist revolutionaries through history who worked to achieve what they believed was genuine class-consciousness-raising education through the traditional organizations of the working class.

For Marxists, the question of education does not cease after a successful working class revolution. The mode of production, which forms the base of society, has an overpowering grip on the population's consciousness. The values of those living within a capitalist mode of production are directly constructed around beliefs in individualism, profit-seeking and competitiveness. In addition, many workers will not be educated enough to posses the skills needed to control society, as Marxism perceives they would need to, when democratic control is handed over to them. For these new consciousness-raising processes to occur, Marx predicted the need for an essential time of transition:

> We are dealing here with a communist society, not as it has developed on its own foundations, but on the contrary, just as it emerges from capitalist society. In every respect, economically, morally, intellectually, it is thus stamped with birth-marks of the old society from whose womb it has emerged. (1974:346)

During this transition, as it becomes more and more unnecessary, the state will wither away and will herald 'a more advanced phase of communist society' (Marx 1976:614). Within the period of transition, education would be of great importance. I will describe later in this chapter how the Marxists of the Russian Revolution believed that they were in the process of this transition and what measures they undertook through their education policy.

So far in the chapter, I have shown the challenges for Marxists in education. The challenges exist in three main phases: education before the revolution, education during the transition and, finally, education in a communist society. In all these phases, literacy teaching takes a central position.

Literacy, Robert Owen and a 'New Education'

Marx wrote relatively few extended texts on education, but in order to understand classic Marxist perspectives about the teaching of literacy it is important to study his conception of polytechnic education and his debt to Robert Owen, the great nineteenth-century reformer. I discussed Owen in Chapter 7 when I explored Marx and Paulo Freire's conception of praxis.

Throughout the book, I have contrasted Marxist ideas with those of social democratic liberal reformers. However, I have maintained that many Marxists were not, and are not, against reform. Indeed, Marx himself regarded the struggles for reform as a powerful way to unite the working class and hasten the process of social revolution (Small 2005). Small (2005) attributes Marx's belief in the benefits of reform (including educational reform) to the transitional nature of change from capitalism to socialism after a revolution, which I raised earlier in this chapter. For Small 'education has a degree of autonomy which allows its form to persist for at least some period beyond transformation in the social relations of production. All the more reason, one might conclude, to commit one self to reform in education before a general transformation of society' (2005:98). This is important, as it suggests that despite the grip the ruling class has upon the superstructures of society, like schooling, forms of education within capitalism can have a positive effect on the development towards a socialist society. It explains why in 1866 Marx contributed to the resolution to the Geneva congress, putting forward plans for polytechnic education for the working class under a capitalist regime and by so doing contributing to our understanding of Marx's approach to education.

In 1864, The International Workingmen's Association was established. It was later to be renamed the First International. This organization unified socialist movements across Europe and the United States and Marx sat on its general council. The International held its very first congress in Geneva in 1866 and Marx was charged with preparing resolutions to be adopted by the congress. The resolution on child labour was effectively a programme for education, for, although approving child labour in a controlled form, it formulated a policy for school instruction which was based on Marx's idea for polytechnic schooling and which arguably owed a debt to the work of Robert Owen and his New Lanark schools. In *Capital* Marx discusses polytechnic schooling in more detail and refers to Owns work as 'education for the future'.

Robert Owen came to his riches and wealth from the impact of the Industrial Revolution. He was self-educated and by the age of 21 was a manager of a successful cotton mill in Manchester. His circle included scholars and business people and he was greatly influenced by the works of Rousseau, Helvetius and Godwin. As I have already described in Chapter 7, Owen possessed a belief in a form of materialism that regarded people as being shaped entirely by social circumstances. A good or 'correct' education could potentially provide everyone with a desirable character and this would change the way society operated. For Owen, education could solve all the social problems he saw around him. Yet, his beliefs constructed working people as passive objects in his scheme for change. They had no role to play in how society could be transformed. His publications addressed the ruling class in the vain hope of convincing them of the way society can be transformed without any form of class struggle. For Marxists, this made Owen idealist and utopian.

In 1800, Owen became a part-owner and the manager of the New Lanark cotton mills in Scotland. He embarked on an extraordinary set of reforms that had education at their heart. He began by stopping the employment of children under 10 in his factories; improving housing; lowering the cost of food and clothing for his workers by buying directly from sources and then selling to his workers. He also tried to reduce crime and drunkenness by attempting to reason with the perpetrators. Education took a central place in these reforms and he established his schooling in three age-related sections: the infant school for children from 18 months to 5 years; the day school for children from 6 until 10 and the evening school for those between 10 and 20. This last section was held after working hours.

There is little doubt that many of the principles and practices of Owen's schools look forward thinking even for today. These principles included some of the following:

- There were no punishments or rewards.
- A mix of mental and physical activities were a consistent feature.

- The education that the children were to receive was focused upon the encouragement of curiosity about their environment.
- The children were to learn from real resources and objects rather than through the medium of books. (Castle and Wustenburg 1979)

Particularly in his infant schools 'children were not to be annoyed with books; but were to be taught the uses of nature or qualities of common things around them' (Owen 1969:71). Astonishingly, Owen was a strong believer that children were not to be taught to read until they were 7 or 8. Owen perceived the written word and written number to be what he called 'artificial signs' which only represented the objects of the real world. He was a staunch believer that children should first of all have time to explore the real world before moving on to representations in literature and other forms of printed text. Interestingly, pressure from the children's parents eventually forced Owen to teach the very young children in his schools to read and to write before they reached the age of 7. Owen describes how his methods of teaching reading included reading from the best texts he could find (there were scant quality books for children at the time) – normally histories or tales of voyages around the world. Owen believed that children should not be expected to have to read texts that they could not understand (Owen 1969). Therefore, in Owen's schools the teacher would read a few sentences, and then stop for discussion to ensure the children had taken in what they had heard.

Owen's work was remarkable for his time and, as I shall show, influenced Marx's perspectives on polytechnic education. However, his work can be categorized as progressive even from a modern-day analysis. It appears to be the beginning of the progressive 'invisible pedagogies' (Bernstein 1996) that have been common in schools in developed countries during much of the middle- and late- twentieth century and are central to social democratic left liberal education perspectives. Owen's work is a form of 'masked pedagogy', an embryo of the forms of pedagogy described in Chapter 6 and falling into my first quadrant. Owen ran a patriarchal system that, although offering his pupils an education that relaxed the criterial and sequential rules (Bernstein 1996) in comparison with harsher forms of Victorian working class education, still made these hierarchical rules explicit. Neither the children nor the parents had much say on how and what the children should be learning. It was an astonishing philanthropy for the time and was both utopian and idealist, but more important, typical of social democratic liberal perspectives, ultimately being thoroughly conservative in its overall objectives.

Polytechnic Education

I want to repeat the assertion that I made at the beginning of this chapter that Marx, unlike Owen, did not believe that society could be transformed by introducing new forms of schooling for children within a capitalist society. He did believe, as I have shown (Small 2005), that education and schooling, as part of the struggle for reform, may help to galvanize the working class, and also that forms of schooling begun under one mode of production may pass into the transition to socialism, meaning that the reform of schooling has some advantages. Generally, however, Marx saw schooling as part and parcel of the totality of the social structures of capitalist modes of production – part of the superstructure that supports the base of society. Yet, he saw the work of Robert Owen as being the germ of future education systems:

> As Robert Owen has shown us in detail, the germ of the education of the future is present in the factory system; this education will, in the case of every child over a given age, combine productive labour with instruction and gymnastics, not only as one of the methods of adding to the efficiency of production, but as the only method of producing fully developed human beings. (Marx 1976:616–18)

Marx's position of polytechnic education was based upon his theoretical view of the division of labour. Small (2005) shows that in *Capital* (1975 CW35:368) Marx cites Hegel: 'By well educated men we understand, in the first instance, those who can do everything that others do'. This citation hints at Marx's belief in an education which enables people to interact with the world in a variety of different ways. Marx indicates, particularly in his earlier writings (1975, CW3), that the form of labour found within modern society negatively affects the capacity of humankind to draw on the whole range of human experience. People are forced to begin to specialize their labour power to accommodate the forms of production necessary and required for economic wealth production and therefore workers become alienated from, what Marx calls, our 'species being' (1975, CW3:275–77) – a state of being in which the individual is able to realize the expanse and capacity of his or her nature.

Marx saw labour as the core of humankind's interaction with nature and vital for the self-realization of humankind. For Marx, we have become alienated from our labour for two reasons. First, the product of a worker's labour belongs not to him or her, but to the ruling class, and second, the capitalist class's interest in extracting surplus value (see Chapter 1) has led to long working hours and to the insistence that work be so specialized that it necessarily limits the complete realization of what a being is capable of. The labour requires only a limited range of skills from the individual worker. For example, this may lead to workers needing only to engage in limited and specific aspects of language and literacy capacity. Work in these circumstances, does not allow the self-realization of individuals, it is oppressive and may damage the mind or the body, crippling the potential development of other potentialities (Castle and Wustenburg 1979).

Marx is certain that it is not industry and technology that have created the problem, but rather their development under capitalist conditions, which have led to enslavement and alienation. Marx wanted a totally developed individual that would be constructed from an education system that united both mental and physical capacities. Mental education refers to learning basic cultural capabilities. These would include reading and writing. There is little detail provided in his work as to how literacy would be taught or how literacy itself was conceptualized, but one has to assume that Marx had in mind a more autonomous model (Street 1984) of literacy, grounded in traditional forms of teaching and learning akin to the pedagogy provided for more privileged sections of society. Later in this chapter, I shall speculate more upon a Marxist form of literacy education, focusing on later Marxist scholarship which also has a more traditional approach to literacy teaching.

Bodily or physical aspects of education are also important to Marx's vision of polytechnic education. Students would be taught the skills necessary to participate in gymnastic, sporting and military activities from the earliest age. Marx also advocated technological training which would be learning to use tools, machines and materials fundamental to systems of production.

Marxism and the 'Relative Autonomy' of Schooling

What is most significant to me about returning to Marx's own work on education and schooling is how relatively little emphasis is placed on what schooling can do to create the kind of change in society advocated by Marx. Even Marx's contribution to the 1866 Geneva resolution and his work on polytechnic education in *Capital* all suggest that, although Marx saw class and the development of class consciousness as being essential to preparing for revolutionary activity, it is absolutely clear that other forms of education were deemed more important – informal education provided by events, particularly those events associated with what Marx saw as the inevitable downfall of each social and economic epoch. His work on polytechnic education is significant in that it does provide a clue to how Marx considers education to be directly linked with aspects of his philosophy – namely the division of labour in capitalist society and its effects upon humankind. Indeed, as we will see later in this chapter, this work was to profoundly influence the later Marxist educators operating in post-revolutionary conditions. However, for Marx, schooling is locked within the social structures of a society and governed by the ruling class. Efforts by well-meaning petit-bourgeois teachers and educators who have been 'born-again' (Freire 1996) into the working class to attempt to incite revolutionary ferment in their students in schools, will do little in comparison with events which will galvanize into action the traditional organizations of the working class.

Modern Marxist or 'Neo-Marxist' educators who have written about critical education and literacy as a tool for change (Apple 1985, Giroux 1983, Carnoy and Levin 1985) have put forward the notion of 'relative autonomy' to overcome the problems of Marx's base and superstructure position of schooling that sees education locked within the superstructures of society. This form of critical literacy pedagogy (discussed earlier in Chapter 7) seeks to find a social space for educators to be 'transformative intellectuals' and allow resistance form their students to the vagaries of living within capitalism. In discussing the question of the possibilities of relative autonomy, Rikowski (1997) quotes Apple:

> . . . there was a dynamic interplay between the political and economic spheres which was found in education. While the former was not reducible to the latter – and, like culture, it had a significant degree of relative autonomy – the role the school plays as state apparatus is strongly related to the core of the problems of accumulation and legitimation faced by the state and a capitalist mode of production in general. (Apple 1985:28–29)

Apple describes here how the political, the cultural and the economic interact, but that – as the work of Willis (1977) on working-class youth using their own cultural resources to provide themselves with power in school, has shown – there were elements of self-selection of cultural forms of resistance that could be found in school settings (Apple 1985) that had a double service of reproducing and contradicting the needs of the social structures of capitalism and demonstrating the relative autonomy of culture. Apple's perspective and relative autonomy, as Rikowski describes:

. . . seemed to offer the best of both worlds; a weak 'economic determinism' (which was held as life line connection with 'traditional Marxism)
and a social space for student resistance, significant teacher politics and
the possibility of radical pedagogic practices within educational sites.
(1997:558),

Others, like Gordon (1989), have criticized the concept of relative autonomy. She questions what 'relative' actually means in terms of its strength.
Furthermore she accuses Apple (1985), and other supporters of relative
autonomy, of oscillating between their efforts to, on the one hand, describe
an all-powerful state increasing its control and power through the efforts
of the New Right in politics in the United States and the United Kingdom,
and working in the interests of capital, and, on the other hand, advocate
for the possibilities for resistance from the students and teachers. A 'dualis-
tic structure agency dilemma' (Rikowski 1997:559) runs though their work.
Sharp (1986) argues that relative autonomy theory suggests that despite
schooling's interconnections with the rest of the capitalist state, it still has
its 'own logic and mode of functioning which warrants separate investiga-
tions' (1986:xv). Schrag (1986) adds to this line of argument by suggesting
that this form of 'liberated Marxism' (p. 49) is more of a way of being liberated from Marxism.The relative autonomy that its advocates, suggest that
schools, teachers and students can 'go beyond the scope of historical materialism' and therefore these people can no longer call themselves Marxists.
Critics suggest that relative autonomy theory is 'a migration into pluralism
and liberalism' (Rikowski 1997:561) and by doing so, pick up the mantle of
social democratic liberalism and consequently the conservatism that this
position entails.

The Revolutionary Party

I now wish to return to classic Marxist positions on education. I do this by
drawing on Marxist revolutionary thinkers and activists and their contention and advocacy of the traditional organizations of the working class to
transform the consciousness of the working class. In doing so, I will not
describe the specific literacy activities found in some of these organizations,
but instead want to contrast this form of education (outside of school) with
that of specifically critical literacy educators and the affordances they claim
their pedagogy has for transforming society. I want to argue that the Marxist
left – the extreme form of the politics I have discussed in this book – looks

to the historical development of capitalism and the working class operating within their own institutions as the central levers to transform society.

Those who are determined to change the consciousness of ordinary people to let them recognize the urgency of the need to transform society have always had one thing in common: a recognition that present societies often privilege certain groups of people over others and that the powerful can oppress the majority through a variety of means. Those in education, whose business concerns the 'changing of consciousnesses' have always been confronted by what has been called the 'subjective factor' (Cannon 1967), or the individual consciousness of those who have the power to transform society as a collective group but who are unable to recognize their collective potential. It was central to the literacy pedagogy of Freire (1996), as I showed in Chapter 7, and is the focus of many of those who espouse critical pedagogy as a strategy for emancipation (Giroux 1987, 1997; McLaren and Jermillo 2007). An important difference within the groups of educationalists on the left is the emphasis that they give to the role of education. As I have shown, Marxism's fundamental position is that 'economic conditions are decisive in shaping the development of society' (Cannon 1967:2). However, Freire (1996) and others, more post-structuralist in their perspectives, take less of an economic determinist position and place greater emphasis on education and its potential for the raising of individuals' critical capability, allowing them to understand how the structures of capitalism operate and recognize the moral bankruptcy of present conditions. Yet, Marxists also argue that, despite the centrality of historical materialism, it is also crucial that when the objective conditions reach a particular maturity the working class must be ready, in terms of their will and consciousness, to undertake the transformation of society.

For many Marxists like Cannon (1967) or Trotsky (1932), the Leninist model of the vanguard party, which was perfected by Lenin in Russia in 1917, is the most efficient way of educating the working class to lead a revolution that will rid the world of capitalism. The party's role was not to assume that its actions to educate its members would lead to the transformation of society on its own, but instead that the party would be able to assist in turning cataclysmic events, formed by the inevitability of capitalism's ultimate failings, to the advantage of socialism.

This vanguard party, as Cannon explains, is based on two factors 'the heterogeneity of the working class and the exceptionally conscious character of the movement for socialism' (1967:2). Cannon describes how revolutionizing oppressed people is a 'complex, prolonged and contradictory affair' (p. 2). In capitalism and class society, the working class becomes stratified and divided and will live in dissimilar conditions. Cannon describes how oppressed peoples have an 'inadequate' (p. 2) culture and that their 'outlook is narrow' (p. 2). In these conditions, the working class do not and cannot arrive en masse at a clear understanding of the conditions and structures within society that cause their oppression. Nor can they learn quickly how they are capable of effectively promoting and protecting their class interests (Cannon 1967). The party can work, through education and action, to put right this irregular self-determination, building a mass party with a clear objective for their struggle.

This was not 'schooling' in the traditional way. It was an education and a changing of consciousness that was to happen within the context of an organization constructed for the working class. The party makes what might be called (borrowing a term from Vygotsky [1978]), a 'revolutionary zone of proximal development'. The party's cadres, who are carefully selected as proven class fighters and who possess an advanced understanding of Marxist perspectives, 'march ahead of the main army' (Cannon 1967:4) but retain appropriate close and class-related links with it. The party becomes the expression of the collective class consciousness of the working class. It is built slowly, its cadres often beginning as a minority voice among the working class, but slowly building as the economic conditions change and confront the people with inevitable choices.

Cannon's reference to the working class's 'narrow outlook' and 'inadequate culture' is mirrored in work on education by the Gramsci whose position on literacy I discussed in Chapter 5. Gramsci was a supporter of the building of a revolutionary party, yet he also believed in the role of schools as organizations which can contribute, to what he called, 'a war of position'.

Gramsci believed that the working class needed emancipation from bourgeois intellectuals who controlled the schools. He wanted workers to develop their own vision of the world (Borg et al. 2002). As Entwistle (1979) describes, Gramsci wanted a pedagogy and curriculum of a more traditional conservative from. It is for this reason that I have chosen to place Marxist education in quadrant 4 to credit it as advocating a visible pedagogy (Bernstein 1996), distinguishing it again from other forms of left education.

Like Cannon's perspective (1967), but unlike many critical literacy pedagogues, Gramsci saw workers' and peasants' language practices as being inadequate. He wanted the oppressed to form and engage in what he saw as being truths discovered by the ruling class of which he considered valuable. Like Lenin, in a post-revolutionary society, he considered the traditional view of academic standards needed to be maintained for workers. He was thought to have glorified didactic pedagogy (Borg et al. 2002).

What differentiates Gramsci from proponents of more classic forms of Marxism, brought to life by revolutionaries like Lenin and Trotsky and expounded by Cannon (1967), is his contention that most revolutions needed to proceed by a 'war of position' that is fought over a long period within the superstructure – in education in the schools and elsewhere. This war of position entails a struggle over meanings and ideas and will precede what Gramsci calls the 'war of manoeuvres', which was a revolutionary war fought at the barricades. He appears to see the positive revolutionary affordances of schooling which many other Marxists who follow a more classic form of Marxism would deny. The struggle over literacy education is a struggle over meaning and, for Gramsci, the tools of meaning-making were the utilization of words that potentially could signify a conceptualization of another form of society. His work has profoundly influenced the ideas of Freire (1996) and other critical pedagogues (Giroux 1987, 1997) because of Gramsci's view that schooling can contribute to revolution.

Lessons from Russia

There have been a number of countries around the world that have broken with capitalism and attempted to construct socialist forms of regime. China, for one, created a new vision of education. However, a study of these new systems would be the subject of another book. So I want to briefly look at the Soviet Union's Marxist position on education as a way to demonstrate their interpretation of Marxism and schooling.

The Russian Marxist revolutionary Lenin did not share Gramsci's vision of the essential need for prerevolutionary education. Lenin invariably chose political activism and the building of a mass revolutionary party over a gradual enlightenment of the people. He disagreed with arguments that Russia's economic cultural backwardness stood in the way of the revolution by the proletariat (Fitzpatrick 2002). However, as leader of the post-revolution Soviet government he insisted upon the importance of education for all and rejected the creation of proletarian 'caste' schools which would be only for the education of the working class. Some Russian revolutionaries were resentful of learning from bourgeoisie intellectuals. Lenin called this 'Communist conceit'.

His judgement was that people with education were more cultured than people without it. Workers and Communists who pretended that 'bourgeois' culture was inferior to 'proletarian' were simply confusing the issue: the basic cultural task of the Soviet state was to raise the educational level of the masses, and the basic task of Communists was to raise their own cultural level by learning the skills of the bourgeoisie. (Fitzpatrick 2001:8)

As a Marxist, Lenin drew on his understanding of the materialist conception of history (see Chapter 1) to colour how he viewed the development of human societies. As I have shown previously, Marxists conceptualize capitalism as imposing deplorable misery and suffering on many in its relentless pursuit of profit, but, taking an unsentimental and materialist stance, see capitalism as being an important stage of human development which has created enormous opportunities for humanity through its development of science and the arts. Marxists insist that socialism or communism will build on these gains and proceed to smash the class society that fashioned both the progress (which can go no further) and capitalism's own demise. This position was shared by other leading Bolsheviks (see Chapter 1, Trotsky 1980).

Post-Revolutionary Schools

Lenin's sense of the autonomous value of education and culture led him after the 1917 revolution to preserve the old universities and technical schools from the old regime. In the social sciences Lenin wanted to introduce Marxist academics into the universities while at the same time retaining others with differing views.

In schools, the viewpoint of Soviet Marxists was that schooling could never be apolitical. Education was always ideological and that it would be hypocritical to deny it (Fitzpatrick 1979). In 1918 a series of decrees on education were introduced which included the following:

- State control of all private and church schools
- Free compulsory education for all children
- Children to be provided with food, clothing and school materials
- Co-education would be introduced
- The end to grading and examinations
- Abolition of uniforms
- The abolition of hierarchical distinctions among teachers with equal pay for all
- The end of punishments and compulsory homework. (Castle and Wustenburg 1979)

In the 1920s, the commissariat of enlightenment (known by the acronym Narkompros) devised programmes for schools which would embody the polytechnic activity principle. The methods that were used sought to get away from subject teaching and attempted to link the school disciplines into what were called 'complex' themes. In primary schools, reading and writing were taught as separate subjects: 'mastery of the skills of speaking, writing, reading, counting and measurement were to be closely linked with the study of the real world; and arithmetic and Russian language were not be taught as separate subjects' (Korolev et al. 1961).

Literature was seen by the leaders of the Narkompros as being central to developing a child's world view. This was a position that had been strongly influenced by Tolstoy's contention that art has an 'infective power'. Literature was to play a major role in the emotional formation of the new Soviet citizen. Krupskaya, Lenin's wife and one of the main leaders of the Narkompros stated that literature:

> . . . is a mighty means for the creation of a new man, a means for the strengthening of particular emotional feelings, a means for influencing human conduct . . .. (cited in Fitzpatrick 1979:Krupskaya 1926:63)

This view of literature was seen to be hopelessly old-fashioned by certain groups of young Marxist intellectuals. Fitzpatrick (1979) describes how, in reality, the literature that did come to be used in schools was by writers who had been identified in terms of their class affiliations and illustrated the art of particular socio-historical situations. Pereverzev, a leading Marxist academic of the 1920s, described literary studies as being able to give 'a completely clear understanding of the class character of literary works which are being studied'.

Teachers who were not familiar with the work of Dewey (from which many of the ideas of the Narkompros derived) or Marx were completely bewildered (Fitzpatrick 1979) and struggled with teaching the complex themes. The reality in schools was that the 'complex' was taught as a separate subject while an hour was given for writing and arithmetic.

Eventually, inconsistency of approach, confusion and ignorance of how to apply progressive methods led to children and parents becoming discontented with their new education. Peasants complained that schools were not providing their children with a basic education in reading, writing and arithmetic. The 'complex' methods were criticized for teaching things about the real world that could be taught at home. After Lenin's death and power being taken over eventually by Stalin, the Narkompros was forced to revise its primary and secondary programme and in 1927 the first compulsory teaching plans and timetable were issued that made the teaching of subjects compulsory. In effect the complex method was abolished. However, during the first five-year plan, progressive methods became dominant again (Fitzpatrick 1979). Yet traditional methods in secondary education never lost their popularity.

The leaders of the Russian Revolution had not expected their revolution to stop at their borders. Their demands were for world socialism and their hope was that workers would revolt across the world. Instead, Russia became increasingly isolated and was forced to fight wars against armies sent from capitalist governments across Europe. The death of Lenin and the rise of Stalin saw what many Marxists believe (Woods 2008), to be a deformity in a real workers state that had been created by the destruction of capitalism. Yet, the history and work of some Soviet leaders offer invaluable insights into their belief about education and what they hoped to achieve. Alas, events worked against their realization.

In this chapter, I have attempted to demonstrate how classic Marxism views culture and, consequently, literacy as autonomous. This perspective differentiates Marxist left positions from those of the social democratic left. For Marxists, culture – literacy, literature, the arts and the sciences – has been integral to the success of human development through the ages. It has consistently been owned and controlled by the ruling class of each socio-economic epoch. The revolution presents the oppressed with the opportunity to win it for themselves in the ultimate democratic act of the redistribution of wealth in all its forms to everyone. For classic Marxists, education within capitalist societies would be brought to the workers by their experience of objective events that are to be caused by the development and ultimate demise of capitalism. In addition to these events, the working class acting within their own organizations – namely, the vanguard party – would add a form of revolutionary class-based criticality which would lead to class action. Despite Gramsci's vision of schooling in capitalism, classic Marxism generally tends to view its potential for making change as limited. As I have said, Marxism has always placed great credence in the value of learning, particularly in the power of learning from traditional and institutionalized sources, an appreciation of art and culture associated with the ruling class. Gramsci's vision was for the working class to learn for themselves, while Trostky and other Marxist revolutionaries believed that this could only be done after the revolution.

Conclusions

At the beginning of this book I set out its basic aims. I wanted to challenge readers about the political background and objectives of the forms of literacy that they may practice or advocate. Justifications for the need to make such an analysis were the consistent patterns of underachievement in school by working-class children and the unequal social trajectories of persons from different socio-economic backgrounds. The brief history of education offered in 'Introduction' demonstrated, from a class perspective (Ball 2008), how astonishingly class-based society has been in structuring schooling – be it implicit or explicit. From a young age, persons are picked out as part of a mass to spend the rest of their lives labouring in poorly paid, semi-skilled or unskilled employment. In Chapter 1, I demonstrated that the Marxist left would argue that this is the result of the workings of capitalism.

I want to end the book contemplating the importance of teachers and educationalists understanding their role within the typology of teaching I offered in Chapter 4. Progressive literacy practices based around romantic (Freire and Macedo 2001) or critical approaches either ignore class inequalities (as in the case of romantic perspectives) or focus on the affordances of cultural literacy practices at the expense of recognizing class society – often because of a belief in the essential longevity of capitalism with all its vagaries. In this chapter, I intend to draw once again on my typology for literacy teaching, which is based upon Bernstein's (1996) own version for pedagogy. In doing so, I wish to reflect upon the middle class and, arguably, conservative nature of literacy practice that is part of an emancipatory and equity discourse. I will argue that this discourse is typical in political terms of the invisible progressive pedagogy that Bernstein (1996) describes and that it is part of a history of education's role in deflecting attention away from more radical left perspectives for the transformation of society.

Identity Investments

Janks contends that 'much work in critical literacy has been done by people whose own identity investments have formed their critical literacy projects' (2010:207). For her it was her own race and nationality and her 'shame in the face of radicalized injustices of apartheid' (2010:206). For others, Janks informs her readers, it may be feminism, concerns about masculinity, class-based consciousness or rejection of heteronormativity. It is 'our own commitments' which 'are often the starting point for the work we do in teaching and research' (2010:206). I feel this is well-said and is central to the argument of this book and, indeed, to the arguments made by many of the left-wing exponents of literacy education. Yet, I want to argue that, from a Marxist left perspective, it is the identity investments for the self-proclaimed radical elements of the middle layers (the petit bourgeoisie) of society which also contribute to the prolongation of inequalities in education and in the wider society.

As I showed in Chapter 4, those whom Bernstein (1996) calls the middle class, are those who establish the structures, discourses and rules within our schools. Two main factions of the middle class have long argued over the pedagogies employed in schools. The middle class advocates of what Bernstein calls progressive pedagogy support a strong role for the state and the growth in public expenditure. For this, as Bernstein informs us, is the ground and opportunity for their reproduction and advancement. The right-wing, or conservative, elements of the middle class support visible pedagogy, or more traditional forms of teaching and learning models. This faction of the middle class is drawn from the economic sector and the entrepreneurial professions and is opposed to growth in public expenditure. Thus, there are opposing 'material and symbolic (discursive) interests' (Bernstein 2003:212) between each. Yet, as Bernstein shows, both factions of this one middle class have their own cultural and class interests at heart, both are pursuing the means for their own social and class reproduction. Most of the debate around education, schooling and pedagogy exists within a single class frame. What appear to be binary divisions in education practice and ethos are in fact contained far more within singular socio-economic sources. So, Janks is quite right to declare that in the field of literacy education one draws on one's identity investments, or what a Marxist would call class interests to sculpt the pedagogy for our children. However, as I have said, despite the seemingly passionate and political content of divisions in belief about education, much of the public debate lies within the middle class. The debates circulate within the confines of what Marxists perceive as class society and capitalism, neither side of the debate advocates its destruction. With this, drawing on Bernstein, one can see that forms of progressive education may not always be as progressive for the working class as it is for the petit bourgeoisie.

This is further echoed by recent research (Rockey 2010) that suggests that there are many in the world who believe themselves to be more left wing than they actually are. Using a large-scale cross-country survey, the researchers compared those who declared themselves to be left wing with those who are, on an objective measure, really left wing. Questions were asked about their political self-perception; whether they thought they were right- or left-wing. Then they were asked their views about particular issues. The results were surprising. The data showed that those who were educated to a higher standard were less accurate as to how they perceived their ideology. 'Higher levels of education are associated with being less likely to believe oneself to be right wing, while simultaneously associated with being in favour of increased inequality' (p. 13). It is my contention that being a progressive educator, following the theoretical framework that Bernstein has left (1996), may not necessary make one as left wing as one may believe. Entrenched class identity and the 'identity investments' that one can feel compelled to make may cast doubtson the legitimacy of those who claim leadership of the oppressed. While examining the work of Marxist and Neo-Marxist critical literacy pedagogues, I have shown the extent of the importance that these writers and practitioners gave to demanding the assurance that the leadership in radical critical literacy programmes or in revolutionary situations must experience a profound change in identity – an 'Easter experience'. Drawing on Walker (1980), I criticized Freire (1996) in Chapter 7 for the overall naivety of his belief in the reliability and consistency of the good will and feeling of moral imperative that these leaders and teachers possess to successfully lead the oppressed to their emancipation. Many Marxists demand the formation of a proletarian party to lead the working class to transform society (Cannon 1967). They too are adamant about those who lead.

> The vanguard party cannot be proclaimed by sectarian fiat or be created over-night. Its leadership and membership are selected and sifted out by tests and trials in the mass movement, and in the eternal controversies and sharp conflicts over the critical policy questions raised at every turn of the class struggle. It is not possible to step over, and even less possible to leap over, the preliminary stage in which the basic cadres of the party organise and reorganise themselves in preparation for . . . winning over the broad sections of the masses. (Cannon 1967)

This position on the teachers and leaders of the oppressed sections of society is in contrast to post-structuralist and social democratic liberal critical literacy educationalists whose 'identity investments' (Janks 2010:205) appear rather modest in comparison. It could be argued that the list of single-issue reasons for teachers to engage in exploring language, discourse and power that, for example, Janks provides, although being noble and understandable, atomizes the source of motivations into the subjective, ignoring the objective conditions created from a central source of oppression – capitalism. Janks' account of the teacher's role also does not insist on any other change in identity, other than recognizing the 'identity investments' that are made by some of the exponents of this form of critical pedagogy. In exploring the spectrum of left perspectives on the teaching of literacy, which have an undeclared general political aim for their work, one is compelled to conclude that post-structuralist-based critical literacy takes a more right-wing and conservative position than some others perspectives I have discussed in this book.

Deflecting the Political Gaze

In my opening chapter, I discussed the history of education from the early nineteenth century onwards. I have been particularly interested in the actions of successive Labour governments in the United Kingdom. This is because the Labour Party was originally formed in the nineteenth century to represent the voice of the trade unions and has been the traditional party of the working class. One might argue that it has at certain times in its history had members who considered themselves politically left-wing or socialist. Indeed, after the Second World War many in the Labour Party were determined to introduce common ownership of the means of production through nationalization of many of the heavy industries in the United Kingdom. Such policies have been the backbone of solid moves towards socialism, galvanizing forces away from a market-owned and controlled economy. Yet, after Labour lost the general election in Britain in 1951, what has been called the 'sickness of Labourism' (Miliband 1972) took hold of the party. This was a period when left-wing aspiration in the Labour party was thwarted by elements on the right of the party who were working to break Labour's commitments to nationalization and common ownership.

Until this time, many in the Labour Party wanted to shape the future of Britain through nationalization and envisaged health care and education reform as providing 'safety nets and opportunities, but not as agencies for the fundamental re-shaping of society' (Jones 2003:50). As I showed in 'Introduction', Anthony Crosland's vision of Britain saw equal opportunity in education as a way to increase the social capacities of the working class, creating greater chances of social mobility (Crosland 1956, Jones 2003). It was through this argument that he called for secondary education to be both universal and equal, ending selection and moving to non-segregated comprehensive education. We now know that the measures for the move away from segregation by ability turned out to be at best rather half-hearted with a timetable for change that was opaque and slow (Jones 2003, Ball 2008). As Jones (2003) shows, there was a 'rhetoric of urgency' (p. 51) with a relaxed timetable and ideologically most of the reformers still believed in division by ability (Young 1958) as the best way to school children.

However, the point I wish to make here is that education reformers from arguably left political sources have often argued for education as a lever for fundamental change as an alternative to policies and actions which are more traditionally thought to enable the transformation of society. As Hatcher (2006) reminded us in 'Introduction', despite reform to the education system and the expansion of the welfare state, levels of inequality still persist in education and the wider society with a clear correlation between social class and educational attainment. One may wish argue, as many on the Marxist left continue to do, that education remains part of the superstructure of society and so offers support to the function of the base of society. One may tamper with it, introducing levels of criticality into the literacy curriculum, offering well-meaning and romantic notions about the power of literature on the personality, but the base of society will still function. Crosland and the Labour Party's switch to educational reform in favour of more fundamental shifts in the power structures of the economy appears now to be a compromise, a conservative alternative to serious transformation of society through wealth distribution. I believe this policy also demonstrates the limitations of educational reform and policy as a means for fundamental change. Changes to education that appear to favour working class members of society can be conceptualized as a social democratic liberal compromising action, diverting and deflecting attention from actions that have more transformative affordance. Furthermore, the actions of a 'left' Labour Party demonstrate the importance of leadership that can genuinely represent the class they were created to serve. Such compromising actions are the tragedy behind many defeats for the working class in recent history.

Literacy on the Left

At the end of this book, it only seems fair to describe what I believe teachers might be doing in their classrooms to further the struggle for change in the way the left has advocated since the days of the French Legislative Assembly of 1791. This must depend on where in the political spectrum individual teachers and educationalists place themselves. One needs to consult my typology of literacy practices and scrutinize the aims and objectives of the practices found within the quadrants. This was the main objective of writing this book.

Teachers are hard-working and caring professionals, many of whom are determined to help all children improve their life chances. I believe passionately that teachers can make a difference to people's lives through their teaching about language and literacy. I personally favour the view that introducing children to literature, art, the humanities and the sciences is the greatest gift that teachers can provide for their students. These areas of study represent the rich fruits of human intellectual development and, yes, I believe they potentially can help sculpt the character of those who study them in ways that can lead to better societies, perhaps following what Gramsci envisaged. It is no accident that the schooling of children from the ruling class in the most expensive private schools is still based around this classical humanist position. I have always advocated progressive methods, as can be seen by the description of some of my own work in Chapter 6. This involves practice that has an invisible pedagogic character, but privileges the positive affordances of reading literature written by great minds. Indeed, the forms of progressive practice advocated (but not always followed through in the classroom) in early post-revolutionary Russia would be my favoured perspective. Yet, my own position would be a purely romantic (Freire and Macedo 1987) perspective if I believed that this alone can help transform society into a fair and equitable state of affairs. In my opinion, teachers need to do more than just teach these subjects. I fear that forms of left literacy pedagogy that sit in quadrant 1 of my typology and describe themselves as 'critical literacies' are embedded in pessimism about the future of society. They are influenced by a form of 'capitalist realism' (Fisher 2009) and their compromise position is to offer compensatory critical capabilities to help overcome capitalism's excesses. This, too, is not enough, and in pursuing this form of critical literacy, some teachers may omit the texts which represent the highest achievements of humankind and belong in the possession of all – indeed, this was Bernstein's (1996) fear.

My typology of literacy pedagogy, that I have drawn from the work of Bernstein (1996) and the later work of Bourne (2004), does not claim to be a thorough classification of the forms of teaching that takes place in schools around the United Kingdom and elsewhere. It simply begins the task of understanding, politically, the different manifestations of literacy teaching around and its social class assumptions. It seems particularly powerful to consider adding a circle around the four quadrants in Figure 3 of Chapter 4 and marking it 'capitalism'. This is because I want to argue that all the pedagogies that are included in the four quadrants are potentially enriching and empowering for students within the context of an alternative political base which many on the left have envisaged. Within the economic and social boundaries of capitalism, those that are given the opportunity to practice, are in many ways contributing to the sustenance of this status quo and that other factors outside of schooling may have greater impact on the possibilities for change.

I was thrilled to read of the work of Chris Searle who sits in quadrant 3 of my typology. In his teaching, he was able to combine the recognition of the importance of children gaining access to powerful texts for both their beauty and the social affordances they provide, while simultaneously validating working class consciousness for his students in a way that facilitated the formation of class-informed critical literacy abilities. However, Hatcher's (2007) (see Chapter 7) insights into why this form of pedagogy is so rare today provide those on the left who favour change with an opportunity to reconsider a teacher's role in making this transformation.

Hatcher is right, I believe, to encourage teachers to also be politically active outside the classroom if they favour left politics. His belief in the power of political and economic events and developments in society, alongside solidarity of teachers in trade unions and associations, creates a powerful cocktail for change. Activist teachers, positioned physically close to working class students in schools, and aligned with other sections of the working-class in trade unions, have an enormous part to play. It may be here that transformative forms of education have the most power. Teachers' professional involvement in campaigns for better conditions, resources and pedagogy raises their own consciousness. It also can raise the consciousness of their students, who witness their teachers' involvement in this form of struggle which focuses their mind on the causes for which they fight.

Literacy and language education plays a crucial role in both conservative, social democratic liberal and Marxist accounts of effective pedagogy. Politics defines the approach that is taken in schools. I hope that by reading this book, despite the complexity of many of the arguments, readers will have understood their own political position and their motivations in attempting to establish a particular form of literacy teaching in schools. Literacy education works dialectically with change and development. This means that literacy teaching is important for human development and change, but it may also be change that defines the literacy teaching which will eventually lead to the liberation that many on the left desire.

Bibliography

Adams, M. (1996). *Beginning to Read: Thinking and Learning about Print*. Cambridge, MA: MIT Press.

Ainley, P. (1993). *Class and Skill. Changing Divisions of Knowledge and Labour*. London: New York: Cassell.

Albright, J. and A. Luke (2009). *Pierre Bourdieu and Literacy Education*. Abingdon, UK: Routledge.

Alexander, R., J. Rose and C. Woodhead (1992). *Curriculum Organisation and Classroom Practice in Primary Schools*. London: HMSO.

Allman, P. (2001). *Revolutionary Social Transformation: Democratic Hopes, Political Possibilities and Critical Education*. Westport, CT: Bergin and Garvey.

Althusser, L. (1971). 'Ideology and the Ideological State Apparatuses' in *Lenin and Philosophy and Other Essays*. London: New Left Books.

Apple, M. (1985). *Education and Power*. London: Ark Paperbacks.

—. (2004). *Ideology and Curriculum,* Third Edition. New York: RoutledgeFalmer.

Arnold, M. (1864/1969). 'A French Eton, or Middle Class Education and the State', in *Matthew Arnold and the Education of the New Order*. P. Smith and G. Summerfield (eds). Cambridge: Cambridge University Press.

Atkinson, E. (2002). 'The Responsible Anarchist: Postmodernism and Social Change'. *British Journal of Sociology of Education,* 23 (1): 73–87.

Badiou, A. (2001). 'On Evil: An Interview with Alain Badiou'. *Cabinet,* Issue 5, *Evil* Winter 2001/2, www.cabinetmagazine.org/issues/5/alainbadiou.php (accessed on June 2010).

Bagley, W. (1911). *Classroom Management*. New York: Macmillan.

Bailey, R. (2001). 'Overcoming Veriphobia – Learning to Love Truth Again'. *British Journal of Educational Studies,* 49 (2): 159–72.

Ball, S. J. (2008). *The Education Debate*. London: The Policy Press.

Barnes, D. (1988). 'The Politics of Oracy', in *Oracy Matters*. M. Maclure (ed.). Maidenhead, UK: Open University Press.

Barton, D. (1994). *Literacy: An Introduction to the Ecology of Written Language*. Oxford: Blackwell.

Barton, D. and M. Hamilton (1998). *Local Literacies: Reading and Writing in One Community*. London: Routledge.

Beakin, M. (1996). *The Making of Language*. Edinburgh: Edinburgh University Press.

Bearne, E. (2002). *Making Progress in Writing*. London: Routledge.

—. (2006). 'Book Jacket Recommendation', in *Phonics: Practice, Research and Policy*. M. Lewis and S. Ellis (eds). London: Paul Chapman/United Kingdom Literacy Association.

Becker, G. (1964). *Human Capital: A Theoretical and Empirical Analysis with Special Reference to Education*, republished 1975. New York: Columbia University Press.

—. (1976). *The Economic Approach to Human Behaviour*. Chicago: University of Chicago Press.

Beckett, F. (2000). 'Couldn't Do Better'. *Guardian Education*, 19 September 2000.

Bee, B. (1980). 'The Politics of Literacy', in *Literacy and Revolution: The Pedagogy of Paulo Freire*. R. Mackie (ed.). London: Pluto Press.

Belsey, C. (2002). *Poststructuralism: A Very Short Introduction*. Oxford: Oxford University Press.

Benn, R. (2000). 'The Genesis of Active Citizenship in the Learning Society'. *Studies in the Education of Adults*, 32 (2): 241–56.

Bennet, P. G. (1999). 'From Secondary School Blues to Lifelong Learning? Aspects of the Retrospective Reevaluation of Formative Educational Experience by Adults'. *International Journal of Lifelong Education*, 18 (3): 155–74.

Bennett, T., M. Savage, E. B. Silva, A. Warde, M. Gayo -Cal and D. Wright, (2006). *Media Culture: The Social Organisation of the Media Field in Contemporary Britain*. London: British Film Institute.

Berggren, C. and L. Berggren (1975). *The Literacy Process: A Practice in Domestication or Liberation*. London: Writers and Readers Publishing Cooperative.

Berman, S. (2007). 'Understanding Social Democracy', www8.georgetown.edu/centers/cdacs//bermanpaper.pdf —(accessed on 11 August 2007).

Bernstein, B. (1990). *The Structuring of Pedagogic Discourse, Vol. IV Class Codes and Control*. London: Routledge.

—. (1996). *Pedegogy, Symbolic Control and Identity*. London: Taylor and Francis.

—. (2003). 'Social Class and Pedagogic Practice' in *The Structuring of Pedagogic Discourse, Vol. IV: Class, Codes and Control*. London: Routledge.

Best, G. (1973). *Mid-Victorian Britain 1851–1875*. New York: Schocken Books.

Blair, T. (1998). *The Third Way: New Politics for the New Century*. London: Fabian Society.

Borg, C., J. Buttigieg, P. Mayo (eds) (2002). *Gramsci and Education*. Lanham, MD:, Rowman and Littlefield Publishers.

Bourdieu, P. (1977). *Outline of a Theory of Practice*. Cambridge: Cambridge University Press.

—. (1984). *Distinction*. R. Nice (trans.). New York: Routledge.

—. (1986). 'The Forms of Capital', in *Handbook of Theory and Research for the Sociology of Education*. J. G. Richardson (ed.), pp. 241–58. New York: Greenwood Press.

—. (1991). *Language and Symbolic Power*, J. B. Thompson (ed.), trans G. Raymond and M. Adamson . Cambridge: Polity Press.

Bourdieu, P. and J. C. Passeron (1977). *Reproduction in Education, Society and Culture*. London: Sage.

Bourne, J. (2004). 'Framing Talk: Towards a 'Radical Visible Pedagogy', in *Reading Bernstein, Researching Bernstein*. J. Muller, B. Davies and A. Morais (eds). London: Routledge Falmer.

Bowles, S. and Gintis, H. (1976). *Schooling in Capitalist America: Educational Reform and the Contradictions of Economic Life*. London: Routledge and Kegan Paul.

Broccoli, A. (1972). *Antonio Gramsci e l'educazione come egemonia*. Florence: La Nuova Italia.

Brooks, M. (2007). 'Historical Materialism', in *What is Marxism*. M. Brooks, R. Sewell and A. Woods (ed.). London: Wellred Books.

Buckingham, D. (2000). *After the Death of Childhood: Growing up in the Age of Electronic Media*. Cambridge: Polity.

Cannon, J. P. (1967). 'The Revolutionary Party and Its Role in the Struggle for Socialism'. *International Socialist Review*, 28 (5): 1–15.

Carnoy, M. and H. Levin (1985). *Schooling and Work in the Democratic State*. Stanford, CA: Stanford University Press.

Carrington, V. and A. Luke (1997). 'Literacy and Bourdieu's Sociological Theory: A Reframing'. *Language and Education*, 11 (2): 96–112.

Castles, S. and W. Wustenburg (1979). *The Education of the Future: An Introduction to the Theory and Practice of Socialist Education*. London: Pluto Press Limited.

Cole, M. (1983). 'Contradictions in the Educational Theory of Gintis and Bowles', *The Sociological Review*. 31(3): 471–88

—. (2008). *Marxism and Educational Theory: Origins and Issues*. Abingdon, UK: Routledge.

—. (2009). *Critical Race Theory and Education: A Marxist Response*. New York: Palgrave Macmillan.

Cole, M., D. Hill, P. McLaren and G. Rikowski (2001). *Red Chalk: On Schooling, Capitalism and Politics*. Brighton, UK: The Institute for Education Policy Studies.

Cole, M. (ed.) (2006). *Education, Equality and Human Rights: Issues of Gender, 'Race', Sexuality, Disability and Social Class*, Second Edition. Oxfordshire: Routledge.

Coles, G. (2000). *Mis-Reading Reading: The Bad Science That Hurts Children*. Portsmouth, NH: Heineman.

Comber, B. (2001). 'Critical Literacy and Local Action: Teacher Knowledge and a "New" Research Agenda', in *Negotiating Critical Literacies in Classrooms*. B. Comber and A. Simpson (eds). London: Lawrence Erlbaum Associates.

Connolly, R. (1980). 'Freire, Praxis and Education', in *Literacy and Revolution: the Pedagogy of Paulo Freire*. R. Mackie (ed.). London: Pluto Press.

Cook-Gumperz, J. (1986). *The Social Construction of Literacy*. Cambridge and New York: Cambridge University Press.

Cordon, R. (2000). *Literacy and Learning through Talk: Strategies for the Primary Classroom*. Buckingham: Open University Press.

Crosland, A. (1956). *The Future of Socialism*. London: Jonathon Cape.

Cusick, P. (1983). *The Egalitarian Ideal and the American School*. New York: Longman.

D'Amato, P. (2006). *The Meaning of Marxism*. Chicago: Haymarket Books.

Davies, S. (1996). 'Margaret Thatcher and the Rebirth of Conservatism' (July 1993). *On Principle Ashland*. Ashbrook Center for Public Affairs.

Dawes, L. (2005). 'Speaking, Listening and Thinking with Computers', in *Teaching, Speaking and Listening in the Primary School*, Second Edition. E. Grugeon, L. Hubbard, C. Smith and L. Dawes (eds). London: David Fulton.

Dawes, L. and C. Sams (2004). *Talk Box: Speaking and Listening Activities For Learning at Key Stage 1*. London: David Fulton.

Denison, E. F. (1962). *The Sources of Economic Growth in the United States and the Alternatives Before Us*. New York: Committee for Economic Development.

Dennis, N., Henriques, F. and Slaughter, C. (1956). *Coal Is Our Life*. London: Eyre and Spottiswoode.

Department for Education and Employment (1998). *The National Literacy Strategy: Framework for Teaching*. London: DfEE.

—. (2000). 'Inner-City Schools Improve Faster to Narrow the Literacy and Numeracy Gap as Test Results Confirm Government Target'. DfEE press release, 20 September 2000.

Department of Education and Science (1988). *Report of Enquiry into the Teaching of English Language* (Kingman Report). London: HMSO.

—. (1989). *English for Ages 5 to 16* (Cox Report). London: HMSO.

Department of Education and Skills (2004). *Five Year Strategy for Children and Learners*. London: HMSO.

—. (2006). *Report of the Teaching and Learning in 2020 Review Group (Gilbert Report)*. London: DfES.

—. (2006). *Independent Review of the Teaching of Early Reading*. London: DfEE.

Derrida, J. (1976). *Of Grammatology*. Baltimore, MD: Johns Hopkins University Press.

Dieterich, H. (2006). *Der Sozialismus Des 21. Jahrhundrerts*. Berlin: Homilius.

Dreeben, R. (1968). *On What is Learned in School*. Reading. MA: Addison-Westley.

Dudley-Marling, C. and S. Murphy (2001). 'Changing the Way We Think about Language Arts'. *Language Arts*, 78: 574–78.

Eagleton, T. (1976). *Marxism and Literary Criticism*. London: Routledge.

—. (2000). *The Idea of Culture*. Oxford: Blackwell.

Education, Science and Arts Committee (ESAC) (1991). *Standards of Reading in Primary Schools*, Third Report. Vol. 1 (May), pp. 261–8.

Ehri, L. C. (1987). 'Learning to Read and Spell Words'. *Journal of Reading Behaviour*, 19: 5–31.

—. (1995). 'Phases of Development in Learning to Read Words by Sight'. *Journal of Research in Reading*, 18 (2): 116–25.

Engels, F. (1970). 'The Part Played by Language in the Transition from Ape to Man', in *Selected Works Vol. 3, K. Marx and F. Engels (1970)*. Moscow: Progress Press.

Ennals, P. (2004). *Child Poverty and Education*. London: National Children's Bureau.

Entwistle, H. (1979). *Antonio Gramsci: Conservative Schooling for Radical Politics*. London: Routledge & Kegan Paul.

Fairclough, N. (1992). *Critical Language Awareness*. Harlow, UK: Addison Wesley, Longman Limited.

—. (2001). *Language and Power*, Second Edition. Harlow, UK: Pearson Education.

—. (2002). 'Editorial: Language in New Capitalism'. *Discourse and Society*, 13 (2): 163–6.

Fisher, M. (2009). *Capitalist Realism: Is There No Alternative?* Ropley, UK: Zero Books.

Fitzpatrick, S. (2002). *Education and Social Mobility in the Soviet Union 1921–1934*, paperback edition. Cambridge: Cambridge University Press.

Fitzsimmons, P. and M. Peters (1994). 'Human Capital Theory and the Industry Training Strategy in New Zealand'. *Journal of Education Policy*. 9 (3): 245–66.

Fives, A. (2008). *Political and Philosophical Debates in Welfare*. Basingstoke, UK: Palgrave Macmillan.

Floud, J., A. H. Halsey and F. M. Marton (1956). *Social Class and Educational Opportunity*. London: Heinemann.

Foucault, M. (1966). *The Order of Things*. London: Tavistock

—. (1979a). *Power, Truth, Strategy*. M. Morris and P. Patton (eds). Sydney: Feral Publications.

—. (1979b). *Discipline and Punish*. Harmondsworth, UK: Penguin.

—. (1980). *Power/Knowledge: Selected Interviews and Other Writings 1972–1977.* C. Gordon (ed.). Brighton, UK: Harvester Press.

—. (1984). 'The Order of Discourse', in *Language and Politics*. M. Shapiro (ed.). Oxford: Blackwell.

Freire, P. (1973). 'Education, Liberation and the Church', in *Study Encounter,* 9 (1): 2.

—. (1976). *Education: The Practice of Freedom*. London: Writers and Readers Publishing Cooperative.

—. (1985). *The Politics of Education*. London: Macmillan.

—. (1996). *The Pedagogy of the Oppressed*. London: Penguin.

Freire, P. and Macedo (1987). *Literacy: Reading the Word and the World*. London: Routledge.

Fukuyama, F. (1992). *The End of History and the Last Man*. New York: Free Press.

Further Education Unit (1987). *Relevance Flexibility and Competence*. London: HMSO.

Gee, J. P. (1996). *Social Linguistics and Literacies: Ideology in Discourses*, Second Edition. London and Bristol, UK: Taylor and Francis.

—. (2001). 'What is Literacy', in *Becoming Political too: New Readings and Writings on the Politics of Literacy Education*. P. Shannon (ed.). Portsmouth, NH: Heinemann.

Giddens, A. (1998). *The Third Way: The Renewal of Social Democracy*. Cambridge: Polity Press.

Giddens, A. (2000). *The Third Way and Its Critics*. Cambridge: Polity Press.

Gilbert, J. (2008). *Anti-Capitalism and Culture: Radical Theory and Popular Politics*. Oxford: Berg Publishers.

Gillborn, D. and H. S. Mirza (2000). *Educational Inequality: Mapping Race, Class and Gender: A Synthesis of Research Evidence*. London: Office for Standards in Education.

Giroux, H. A. (1981). *Ideology, Culture and the Process of Schooling*. Philadelphia, PA: Temple University Press.

—. (1983). *Theory and Resistance in Education: A Pedagogy for the Opposition*. London: Heinemann Educational Books.

—. (1987). 'Literacy and the Pedagogy of Political Empowerment', in *Literacy: Reading the Word and the World*. P. Freire and D. Macedo (eds). London: Routledge.

—. (1997). *Pedagogy and the Politics of Hope: Theory, Culture and Schooling*. Boulder, CO: Westview Press.

Glass, D. V. (ed.) (1954). *Social Mobility in Britain*. London: Routledge.

Goldthorpe, J. H. and Marshall, G. (1992). *The Promising Future of Class Analysis: A Response to Recent Critiques, Sociology*. 26 (3): 381–400.

Goouch, K. and A. Lambirth, (2007). *Understanding Phonics and the Teaching of Reading: Critical Perspectives*. Maiden head: Open University Press.

Gordon, L. (1989). 'Beyond Relative Autonomy Theories of the State in Britain'. *British Journal of Sociology of Education*, 10: 435–47.

Gordon, L. (1991). 'Is School Choice a Sustainable Policy for New Zealand?: A Review of Recent Research Findings and a Look to the Future'. *New Zealand Annual Review of Education. Te Arotake a Tau o te Ao o te Mataurnga I Aotearoa*, Hugo Manson (ed.), 4: 9–24.

Goswami, U. (2007). 'Learning to Read Across Languages: The Role of Phonics and Synthetic Phonics', in *Understanding Phonics and the Teaching of Reading: Critical Perspectives*. K. Goouch and A. Lambirth (eds). Maidenhead, UK: Open University Press.

Graff, H. A. (1979). *The Literacy Myth*. New York: Academic Press.

Grainger, T., K. Goouch and A. Lambirth (2005). *Creativity and Writing: Developing Voice and Verve in the Classroom*. Abingdon, UK: Routledge.

Gramsci, A. (1971). *Selections from the Prison Notebooks of Antonio Gramsci*. Q. Hoare and G. Nowell Smith (eds and trans). London: Lawrence and Wishart.

Grant, T. (2002). *History of British Trotskyism*. London: Wellread Books.

Graves, D. (1983). *Writing: Teachers and Children at Work*. Portsmouth, NH: Heinemann.

Grugeon, E., L. Hubbard, C. Smith and L. Dawes (2001). *Teaching, Speaking and Listening in the Primary School*, Second Edition. London: David Fulton.

'Gurney-Dixon Report, The' (1954). *Early Leaving*. London: HMSO.

Gutmann, A. (1987). *Democratic Education*. Princeton, NJ: Princeton University Press.

Hamilton, M., D. Barton and R. Ivanic, (1994). *Worlds of Literacy*. Clevedon: Multilingual Matters.

Hannon, P. (2000). *Reflecting on Literacy Education*. London: RoutledgeFalmer.

Harrison, C. (2006). 'Book Jacket Recommendation', in *Phonics: Practice, Research and Policy*, M. Lewis and S. Ellis (eds). London: Paul Chapman/United Kingdom Literacy Association.

Hatcher, R. (2006). 'Social Class and Schooling: Differentiation or Democracy', in *Education, Equality and Human Rights: Issues of Gender, 'Race', Sexuality, Disability and Social Class*, Second Edition, M. Cole (ed.). Oxfordshire: Routledge.

—. (2007). 'Yes, but how do we get there?' Alternative Visions and the Problem of Strategy'. *Journal for Critical Education Policy Studies*. 5(2): pp. 1–17.

Hatcher, R. and N. Hirtt (1999). 'The Business Agenda behind Labour´s Education Policy', in *Business, Business, Business: New Labour´s Education*. M. Allen et al. (eds). London: Tufnell Press.

Hayek, F. A. (1944). *The Road to Serfdom*. London: Routledge & Kegan Paul.

Heath, S. B. (1983). *Ways with Words: Language, Life, and Work in Communities and Classrooms*. Cambridge: Cambridge University Press.

Hill, D. (2001). 'Equality, Ideology and Education Policy', in *Schooling and Equality: Fact, Concept and Policy*. D. Hill and M. Cole (eds). London: Kogan Page.

—. (2007). 'What Neolibereal Global and National Capitals Are Doing to Education Workers and to Equality – Some Implications for Social Class Analysis', in *Renewing Dialogues in Marxism and Education: Openings*. A. Green, G. Rikowski and H. Raduntz (eds). Basingstoke: Palgrave Macmillan.

Hirsch, D. (2007). *Experience of Poverty and Educational Disadvantage*. London: Joseph Rowentree Foundation.

Hobsbawm, E. (1994). *Age of Extremes: The Short Twentieth Century 1914–1991*. London: Michael Joseph.

Hoggart, R. (1958). *The Uses of Literacy*. Harmondsworth: Penguin

Holborow, M. (1999). *The Politics of English*. London: Sage.

—. (2004). 'Putting the Social Back into Language'. *Studies in Language and Capitalism*, 1: 1–28.

Honey, J. (1997). *Language Is Power: The Story of Standard English and Its Enemies*. London: Faber and Faber.

Hoyles, M. (1977). 'The History and Politics of Literacy', in *The Politics of Literacy*. M. Hoyles (ed.). London: The Readers and Writers Publication Cooperative.

Jaggar, A. M. (1983). *Feminist Politics and Human Nature*. Hemel Hempstead, UK: Rowan and Allanheld/Harvester Press.

James, A. and A. Prout (eds) (1997). *Constructing and Reconstructing Childhood: Contemporary Issues in the Sociological Study of Childhood*, Second Edition. London: Falmer Press.

Janks, H. (2000). 'Domination, Access, Diversity and Design: A Synthesis for Critical Literacy Education'. *Educational Review*, 52 (2): 175–86.

—. (2010). *Literacy and Power*. Abingdon, UK: Routledge.

Jenkins, R. (1992). *Pierre Bourdieu*. London: Routledge.

Johnstone, R. and J. Watson (2003). *Accelerating Reading and Spelling with Synthetic Phonics: A Five Year Follow Up*. Edinburgh: The Scottish Executive Education Department; Insight 4.

—. (2005). 'The Effects of Synthetic Phonics Teaching of Reading and Spelling Attainment: A Seven Year Longitudinal Study'. Available online at www.scotland. gov.uk/ (accessed on 7 January 2011).

Johnston, P. and Costello, P. (2009). 'Principles for Literacy Assessment, in *Approaching Difficulties in Literacy Development: Assessment, Pedagogy and Programmes*. Fletcher-Campbell, J. Solar and G. Reid (eds.) London: Sage.

Jones, K. (2003). *Education in Britain: 1944 to the Present*. Cambridge: Polity press.

Kane, L. (2007). 'The Educational Influences on Active Citizens: A Case Study of Members of the Scottish Socialist Party (SSP)'. *Studies in the Education of Adults*, 39 (1): 54–76.

Kelly, J. (2000). 'Gender and Equality: One hand Tied Behind Us', in *Education, Equality and Human Rights: Issues of Gender, 'Race' Sexuality, Special Needs and Social Class*. M. Cole (ed.). London: RoutledgeFalmer.

Knapp, A. and V. Wright (2006). *The Government and Politics of France*. London: Routledge.

Korolev, F. F., Korneichik, T. D. and Ravkin, Z. I. *Orcherki po istorii sovetskoi shkoly i pedagogiki 1921–1931*. Moscow: Moscow Press.

Krashen, S. (1982). *Principles and Practice in Second Language Acquisition*. Hayward, CA: Alemany Press.

Krashen, S. and T. Terrell (1983). *The Natural Approach: Language Acquisition in the Classroom*. Hayward, CA: Alemany Press.

Krupskaya (1926). *Na putyakh k novoi shkole*. No. 5–6. Moscow: Moscow Press.

Labour Party (1997). *New Labour: Because Britain Deserves Better* (election manifesto). London: Labour Party.

Lambirth, A. (2006). 'Challenging the Laws of Talk: Ground Rules, Social Reproduction and the Curriculum'. *The Curriculum Journal*, 17 (1): 59–71.

—. (2007). 'Social Class and the Struggle to Learn to Read: Using Bernstein to Understand the Politics of the Teaching of Reading', in *Understanding Phonics and the Teaching of Reading: Critical Perspectives*. K. Goouch and A. Lambirth (eds). Maidenhead, UK: Open University Press.

—. (2009). 'Ground Rules for Talk: the Acceptable Face of Prescription'. *The Curriculum Journal*. 20(4), pp. 423–35.

—. (2010). 'Class Consciousness, Power, Identity, and the Motivation to Teach'. *Power and Education*, 2 (2): 209–22.

Lankshear, C. and Knobel, M. (2002). 'New Times! Old Ways?' in *Contextualising Difficulties in Literacy Development: Exploring Politics, Culture, Ethnicity and Ethics.* J. Solar, J. Wearmouth and G. Reid (eds). London: Routledge.

—. (2003). *New Literacies: Changing Knowledge and Classroom Learning.* Buckingham, UK: Open University Press.

—. (2009). 'More than Words: Chris Searle's Approach to Critical Literacy as Cultural Action'. *Race and Class*, 51 59–78.

Lankshear, C. and M. Lawler (1987). *Literacy, Schooling and Revolution.* London: Falmer Press.

Larrain, J. (1979). *The Concept of Ideology.* London: Hutchinson.

Larson, J. and J. Marsh (2005). *Making Literacy Real: Theories and Practice for Learning and Teaching.* London: Sage.

Lather, P. (2001). 'Ten Years, Yet Again: Critical Pedagogy and Its Complicities', in *Feminist Engagements : Reading, Resisting and Revisioning Male Theorists in Education and Cultural Studies.* K. Weiler (ed.). London: Routledge.

Lawlor, S. (1990). *Teachers Mistaught: Training in Theories or Education in Subjects.* London: Centre for Policy Studies.

Lemke, J. L. (1995). *Textual Politics: Discourse and Social Dynamics.* Abingdon, UK: Taylor and Francis.

Lenin, I. (1919). 'The state': A lecture delivered at Sverdlov University, Moscow, 11th June, 1919. London: Modern Publishers.

Levin, B. (2004). 'Media–Government Relations in Education'. *Journal of Education Policy*, 19: 271–83.

Lewis, M. and S. Ellis (eds) (2006). *Phonics: Practice, Research and Policy.* London: Paul Chapman/United Kingdom Literacy Association.

Liston, D. (1988). 'Faith as Evidence: Examining Marxist Explanations of Schooling', *American Journal of Education*, 96: 323–50.

Luke, A. (2009). 'Using Bourdieu to Make Policy: Mobilising Community Capital and Literacy', in *Pierre Bourdieu and Literacy Education.* J. Albright and A. Luke (eds). Abingdon, UK: Routledge.

Luke, A. and P. Freebody (1997). 'The Social Practices of Reading', in *Constructing Critical Literacies: Teaching and Learning Textual Practice.* S. Muspratt, A. Luke and P. Freebody (eds). Sydney: Allen and Unwin.

Luxemburg, R. (1970). *Reform or Revolution.* New York: Pathfinder Books.

Lyotard, J. F. (1993). *The Postmodern Condition: A Report on Knowledge.* Minneapolis, MN: University of Minnesota Press.

Mackie, R. (1980). 'Introduction', in *Literacy and Revolution: The Pedagogy of Paulo Freire.* R. Mackie (ed.). London: Pluto Press.

Macnair, L., S. Evans, M. Perkins, P. Goodwin (2006). 'Inside the Classroom: Three Approaches to Phonics Teaching', in *Phonics: Practice, Research and Policy.* M. Lewis, S. Ellis (eds). London: Paul Chapman/United Kingdom Literacy Association.

Maguire, M. (2001). '*The Cultural Formation of Teachers*'. Class Consciousness: Teachers in the Inner City Journal of Education Policy. Vol. 16, No. 4, 315–331.

Marx, K. (1845). The German Ideology. www.marxists.org/archive/marx/works/1845/german-ideology/ch01a.htm (accessed on 03 January 2011).

—. (1859). A Contribution to the Critique of Political Economy. www.marxists.org/archive/marx/works/1859/critique-pol-economy/preface.htm (accessed on 03 January 2011).

—. ([1869]1977). 'Speech to the Delegation of German Trade Unionists' in *The Thought of Karl Marx*. D. McLellan (ed.). London: Macmillan Press'.

—. (1871). 'Decision of London Conference', in *Selected Works, 2 Vols. K. Marx and F. Engels (1964)*. Moscow: Progress Press.

—. (1974). 'Critique of the Gotha programme' in *The First International and After*. Harmondsworth: Penguin.

—. (1976). *Capital. Vol. 1*. Harmondsworth, UK: Penguin.

Marx, K. and F. Engels (1969). *Selected Works, Vol. 1*. Moscow: Progress Publishers.

—. (1974). *The German Ideology*. C. J. Arthur (ed.). London: Lawrence and Wishart.

—. (1975–2002).*Collected Works*. London: Lawrence and Wishart.

McCallum, I. and G. Readhead (2000). 'Poverty and Educational Performance'. *Poverty*, 106: 14–17.

McCann, P. (ed.) (1977). *Popular Education and Socialisation in the Nineteenth Century*. London: Methuen.

McGuinness, D. (1998). *Why Children Can't Read and What We Can Do about It*. Harmondsworth, UK: Penguin.

McLaren, P. (1987). 'Ideology, Science, and the Politics of Marxian Orthodoxy: A Response to Michael Dale.' *Educational Theory*, 37: 301–33.

—. (2001). 'Postmodernism', in *Red Chalk: On Schooling, Capitalism and Politics*. M. Cole, D. Hill, P. McLaren and G. Rikowski (eds). Brighton, UK: The Institute for Education Policy Studies.

McLaren, P., and N. Jaramillo (2007). *Pedagogy and Praxis in the Age of Empire: Towards a New Humanism*. Rotterdam: Sense Publishers.

McLellan, D. (1980). *The Thought of Karl Marx*, Second Edition. London: Macmillan.

McLellan D. (ed.) (1977). *Karl Marx: Selected Writings*. Oxford: Oxford University Press.

McMurtry, J. (2002). *Value Wars: The Global Market Versus the Life Economy*. London: Pluto Press.

Meighan, R. and I. Siraj-Blatchford (1998). *A Sociology of Educating*, Third Edition. London: Cassell.

Mercer, N. (2000). *Words and Minds: How We Use Language to Think Together*. London: Routledge.

Mercer, N. and Littleton, K. (2007). *Dialogue and the Development of Children's Thinking: A Sociocultural Approach*. Abingdon, UK: Routledge.

Mercer, N., K. Littleton and R. Wegerif (2004). 'Methods for Studying the Processes of Interaction and Collaborative Activity in Computer-based Educational Activities'. *Technology, Pedagogy and Education*, 13 (2): 193–209.

Mercer, N., R. Wegerif and L. Dawes (1999). 'Children's Talk and the Development of Reasoning'. *British Educational Research Journal*, 25 (1): 95–111.

Miliband, R. (1972). *Parliamentary Socialism*, Second Edition. London: Merlin Press.

Mill, J. S. ([1859]1972). *On Liberty* (1956 edition). C. V. Shield (ed.). Indianapolis, IN: Bobbs Merrill Library of Liberts Arts.

National Reading Panel (2000). *Teaching Children to Read*. Washington, DC: NIH Publications.

O'Connor, J. (1984). *Accumulation Crisis*. Oxford: Blackwell.

OECD (2000). *Literacy in the Information Age: Final Report of the International Adult Literacy Survey*. Paris: OECD.

Offe, C. (1985). 'The New Social Movements: Challenging the Boundaries of Intuitional Politics' *Social Research*. 52 (4): 817–68.

Office for Standards in Education (Ofsted) (1996a). *The Teaching of Reading in 45 Inner London Schools*. London: Ofsted Publications.

—. (1996b). *Subjects and Standards: 1994/5*. London: Ofsted Publications.

Olssen, M. and M. Peters (2007). 'Marx, Education, and the Possibilities of a Fairer World: Reviving Radical Political Economy through Foucault' in *Renewing Dialogues in Marxism and Education: Openings*. A. Green, G. Rikowski and H. Radunz (eds). Basingstoke, UK: Palgrave Macmillan.

Olssen, M., J. Codd and A. O'Neil (2004). *Education Policy: Globalisation, Citizenship and Democracy*. London: Sage.

O'Neil, W. (1977). 'Properly Literate' in *The Politics of Literacy*. M. Hoyles (ed.). London: Writers and Readers Publication Cooperative

Owen, R. (1969). 'A New View of Society' in *Robert Owen on Education*. H. Silver (ed.). Cambridge: Cambridge University Press.

—. (1970). *A New View of Society*. V. A. C. Gaterell (ed.). Harmondsworth, UK: Penguin.

Ozga, J. (ed.) (1988). *Schoolwork: Approaches to the Labour Process of Teaching*. Milton Keynes: Open University.

Pahl, R. (1993). 'Does Class Analysis Without Class Theory Have a Promising Future?' *Sociology*. 27(2): 253–58.

Pakulski, J. and Waters, M. (1996). *The Death of Class*. London: Sage.

Parsons, T. (1959). 'The School Class as a Social System: Some of its Functions in American Society'. *Harvard Educational Review*. 29 (4): 297–318.

Perkin, H. (1969). *The Origins of Modern Society, 1780–1880*. London: Routledge.

Pinker, S. (1995). *The Language Instinct*. Harmondsworth, UK: Penguin.

Plant, R. (1991). *Modern Political Thought*. Oxford: Blackwell.

—. (1996). *Modern Political Thought*. Oxford: Blackwell.

Plekhanov, G. (1953). *Art and Social Life*. London: Lawrence and Wishart.

Pollard, A. (1996). *Introduction to Primary Education: For Parents, Governors and Student Teachers*. London: Cassell.

Postman, N. (1973). 'The Politics of Reading' in *Tinker, Tailor . . . .* N. Keddie (ed.). London: Penguin.

Rafferty, F. (1996). 'Labour Gets Back to Basics'. *Times Educational Supplement* (31 May), http://web.lexis.com/executive/ (accessed on November 2006).

Raven, J., J. Court and J. C. Raven (1995). *Manual For Raven's Progressive Matrices and Vocabulary Scales*. Oxford: Oxford Psychologists Press.

Reeder, D. (ed.) (1977). *Urban Education in 19th Century London*. London: Taylor and Francis.

Rentoul, J. (1997). *Tony Blair*. London: Warner Books.

Reuss, J. C. (2000). *American Folk Music and Left-Wing Politics*. Lanham, MD: The Scarecrow Press.

Rikowski, G. (1992). 'Work Experience Schemes and Part time jobs in a Recruitment Crisis'. *British Journal of Education and Work*, 5 (1): 19–46.

—. (1997). 'Scorched Earth: Prelude to Rebuilding Marxist Educational Theory'. *British Journal of Sociology of Education*, 18 (4): 551–74.

—. (2000). 'That Other Great Class of Commodities: Repositioning Marxist Educational Theory'. *BERA Conference Paper*, Cardiff University. 7–10 September

Rockey J. (2010). 'Who Is Left Wing, and Who Just Thinks They Are?'. *Working Paper* No. 9 (23), pp. 1–22. Leicester :University of Leicester Department of Economics.

Rose, J. (2006). *Independent Review of the Teaching of Early Reading.* Nottingham: DFES Publications.

Rosen, H. (1982). 'Out There or Where the Masons Went' in *The Politics of Literacy.* M. Hoyles (ed.). London: Writers and Readers Publishing Coopertaive Society.

Rubenstein, D. (1969). *School Attendance in London 1870–1904.* Hull: University of Hull Press.

Sadovnik, A. R. (2001). 'Basil Bernstein (1924–2000): Sociologist, Mentor and Friend' in *A Tribute to Basil Bernstein 1924–2000.* S. Power, P. Aggleston, J. Brannen, A. Brown, L. Chisholm and J. Mace (eds). London: Institute of Education.

Saussure, F. (1916). *Course in General Linguistics.* W. Baskin (trans. 1974). London: Fontana.

Saville, J. (1977). 'The Welfare State: An Historical Approach', in *Welfare in Action.* M. Fitzgerald, P. Halmos, J. Muncie and D. Zeldin (eds), pp. 4–9. London and Henley: Routledge & Kegan Paul.

Sayers, D. (1979). *Marx's Method: Ideology, Science and Critique in Capital.* Hassocks, UK: Harvester Press.

Scholes, R. (1985). *Textual Power: Literary Theory and the Teaching of English.* London: Yale University Press.

Schrag, F. (1986). 'Education and Historical Materialism'. *Interchange*, 17: 42–52.

Schultz, T. (1960). 'Capital Formation by Education', *Journal of Political Economy*, 68 (6): 571–83.

Schultz, T. (1961). 'Investment in Human Capital', *American Economic Review*, 51 (1): 1–17.

Searle, C. (1998). *None But Our Words: Critical Literacy in Classroom and Community.* Buckingham, UK: Open University Press.

Searle, C. (ed.) (1975). *Classrooms of Resistance.* London: Writers and Readers Publishing Cooperative.

Selleck, R. J. W. (1968). *The New Education: The English Background 1870–1914.* Melbourne: Pitman and Sons.

Sewell, R. (2007). 'Dialectical Materialism', in *What is Marxism?* R. Sewell, M. Brooks and A. Wood (ed.). London: Wellred Books.

Shannon, P. (1989). *Broken Promises: Reading Instruction in 20th Century America.* South Hadley, MA: Bergin & Garvey.

—. (2000). 'A Marxist Reading of Reading Education'. *Cultural Logic.* Vol. 4, No. 1.

—. (2007). 'The Limits of Science in the Phonics Debate', in *Understanding Phonics and the Teaching of Reading: Critical Perspectives.* K. Goouch, and A. Lambirth (eds.). Maiden head: Open University Press.

Shannon, P. (ed.) (2001). *Becoming Political Too.* Portsmouth, NH: Heinemann.

Sharp, R. (1986). 'Introduction', in *Capitalist schooling: Comparative Studies in the Politics of Education.* R. Sharp (ed.). South Melbourne: Macmillan Company of Australia.

Sheehan, P. (2004). 'Postmodernism and Philosophy' in *The Cambridge Companion to Postmodernism.* S. Connor (ed.). Cambridge: Cambridge University Press.

Shonfield, A. (1965). *Modern Capitalism: The Changing Balance of Public and Private Power.* London: Oxford University Press.

Simon, B. (1994). *The State and Educational Change: Essays in the History of Education and Pedagogy.* London: Lawrence and Wishart.

Small, R. (2005). *Marx and Education.* Aldershot, UK : Ashgate.

Smith, G., T. Smith and G. Wright (eds) (1997). *Britain Divided: The Growth of Social Exclusion in the 1980s and 1990s.* London: Child Poverty Action Group.

Snow, C., S. Burns and P. Griffen (1998). *Preventing Reading Difficulties in Young Children.* Washington, DC: National Academy Press.

Soler, J. and R. Openshaw (2007). ' " To be or not to be?" The Politics of Teaching Phonics in England and New Zealand'. *Journal of Early Childhood Literacy,* 7 (3): 333–52.

St Pierre, P. (2000). 'The Call for Intelligibility in Postmodern Educational Research'. *Educational Researcher,* (June/July): 25–8.

Strauss, S. L. and B. Alwerger (2007). 'The Logographic Nature of English Alphabetics and the Fallacy of Direct Intensive Phonics Instruction'. *Journal of Early Childhood Literacy,* 7 (3): 299–319.

Storey, J. (2001). *Cultural Theory and Popular Culture: An Introduction,* Third Edition. Harlow, UK: Pearson Education.

Street, B. V. (1984). *Literacy in Theory and Practice.* Cambridge: Cambridge University Press.

—. (1995). *Social Literacies: Critical Approaches to Literacy in Development, Ethnography and Education.* London and New York: Longman.

Street, B. V. (ed.) (1993). *Cross-Cultural Approaches to Literacy.* London: Cambridge University Press.

—. (ed.) (2003). 'What's "new" in New Literacy Studies? Critical Approaches to Literacy in Theory and Practice'. *Current Issues in Comparative Education,* 5 (2): 1–14.

Street, B. and A. Lefstein (2007). *Literacy: An Advanced Resource Book.* Abingdon, UK: Routledge.

Street, B. V. and Street, J. (1991). 'The Schooling of Literacy', in *Writing in the Community.* D. Barton and R. Ivanic (eds). London: Sage Publications.

Sturt, M. (1970). *The Education of the People.* London: Routledge & Kegan Paul.

Thomas, S. (2000). *Overall Patterns of Achievement* (unpublished working paper on school effectiveness).

Thompson, J. B. (1990). *Ideology in Modern Culture: Critical Social Theory in the Era of Mass Communication.* Stanford, CA: Stanford University Press.

Tomlinson, S. (2005). *Education in Post-Welfare Society,* Second Edition. Maidenhead, UK: Open University Press.

Tooley, J. (1996). *Education Without the State.* London: The Institute of Economic Affairs.

Trotsky, L. ([1924]1973). 'Young People, Study politics!' in *Problems of Everyday Life and Other Writings on Culture and Science.* New York: Pathfinder Press.

—. (1932). *What's Next: Vital questions for the German Proletariat.* July 2010, www.marxists.org/archive/trotsky/germany/1932-ger/index.htm. (accessed on 07 January 2011).

—. (1963) *Leon Trotsky Presents the Living Thoughts of Karl Marx*. London: Fawcett Premier Books

—. (1974). 'The Fabian Theory of Socialism' in *Trotsky's Writings on Britain Vol. 2*. R. Chappell and A. Clinton (eds). London: New Park Publications.

—. (1975). *My Life*. London: Penguin.

—. (1980). 'From Literature to Revolution', in *Leon Trotsky on Literature and Art*. P. N. Siegel (ed.). New York: Pathfinder Press.

Trotsky, L. D. (1980). 'Class and Art', in *Leon Trotsky on Literature and Art*. P. N. Siegel (ed.). New York: Pathfinder Press

Turner, B. (1988). *Status*. Milton Keynes: Open University Press.

Turner, M. (1990). *Sponsored Reading Failure: A Object Lesson*. Warlingham, UK: Education Unit, Warlingham Park School.

van der Berg, S. (2008). *Poverty and Education*. Paris: International Institute of Educational Planning.

van Gosse (2005). *The Movements of the New Left, 1950–1975: A Brief History with Documents*. New York: Palgrave Macmillan.

Vasquez, V. (2005). 'Critical Literacy', in *Making Literacy Real: Theories and Practices for Learning and Teaching*. J. Larson and J. Marsh (eds). London: Sage.

Voloshinov, V. (1973). *Marxism and the Philosophy of Language*. L. Matejka and I. R. Titunik (trans). New York: Seminar Press.

Vygotsky, L. S. (1978). *Mind in Society*. Cambridge, MA: Harvard University Press.

—. (1997). 'The Instrumental Method in Psychology' in *The Collected Works of L. S. Vygotsky*, Vol. 3. *Problems of the Theory and History of Psychology*. New York: Plenum.

Walker, J. (1980). 'The End of Dialogue: Paulo Freire on Politics and Education', in *Literacy and Revolution: The Pedagogy of Paulo Freire*. R. Mackie (ed.). London: Pluto Press.

Wegerif, R., N. Mercer and L. Dawes (1999). 'From Social Interaction to Individual Reasoning and Empirical Investigation of a Possible Socio-Cultural Model of Cognitive Development'. *Learning and Instruction*, 9: 493–516

Wells, G. (1985). 'Preschool Literacy-related Activities and Success in School' in *Literacy, Language and Learning*. D. R. Olson, N Torrance and A. Hildyard (eds). Cambridge: Cambridge University Press.

—. (1986). 'The Language Experience of Five-Year-Old Children at Home and at School' in *The Social Construction of Literacy*. J. Cook-Gumperz (ed.). Cambridge: Cambridge University Press.

West, E. G. (1994). 'Education Without the State'. *Economic Affairs*, 14 (5): 12–15.

Wheen, F. (2006). *Marx's Das Kapital: A Biography*. London: Atlantic Books.

Williams, R. (1983). *Keywords*. London: Fontana.

Willis, P. (1977). *Learning to Labour: How Working Class Kids Get Working Class Jobs*. Farnborough: Saxon House.

Wodak, R. (1996). *The Disorders of Discourse*. Harlow, UK: Longman.

Woods, A. (2008). *Reformism or Revolution: Marxism and Socialism of the 21st Century Reply to Heinz Dieterich*. London: Wellread Books.

World Social Forum (2002). *Charter of Principles*, www.wsfindia.org/?q=node/3 (accessed on July 2010).

Wrigley, T. (2006). *Another School Is Possible*. London: Bookmark Publications.

Wyse, D. and U. Goswami (2008). 'Synthetic Phonics and the Teaching of Reading'. *British Educational Research Journal,* 34 (6): 691–710.

Wyse, D. and M. Styles (2007). 'Synthetic Phonics and the Teaching of Reading: The Debate Surrounding England's "Rose Report"'. *Literacy,* 41 (1): 35–42.

Young, M. and Willmott, P. (1957). *Family and Kinship in East London.* London: Routledge.

Index

Printed in Great Britain
by Amazon.co.uk, Ltd.,
Marston Gate.